GLEN LYON

Kenneth Steven grew up in a writing family. He moved with his parents to Perthshire during primary school days, and it has been the glens, rivers and hills of this heart of Scotland that have inspired much of his poetry and prose. When he first came to Perthshire, there were still the last traces of an older world to be found. The places, people and stories of that world compose the backbone of this novel.

Kenneth Steven travels widely to read from his work, and to facilitate the creative writing of adults and youngsters alike. He has written and presented many programmes for BBC Radio.

GLEN LYON

A NOVEL

Kenneth Steven

BIRLINN

First published in 2013 by
Birlinn Limited
West Newington House
10 Newington Road
Edinburgh
EH9 1QS

www.birlinn.co.uk

ISBN: 978 1 78027 177 4

British Library Cataloguing-in-Publication Data
A catalogue record for this book is available from the British Library

Typeset by Iolaire Tyepsetting, Newtonmore
Printed and bound by Grafica Veneta
www.graficaveneta.com

This novel would not have been written without a grant from the Authors' Foundation. The provision of this allowed me to travel to Iceland in the summer of 2012 to work intensively on the story in absolute quiet. In addition, my stay in Iceland would not have been possible had it not been for the generosity of the Icelandic Writers' Union in providing me with a writers' house in a small community an hour from Reykjavik. And I want to thank the library staff in that community for all their support and kindness over the weeks of my stay. I would like to dedicate this story to them, and to my two Icelandic writer friends, Gyrdir Eliasson and Athalsteinn Asberg.

The man walked over the ice, the stone axe in his hand. And the forest gave way before him. The wind blew him and his feet, booted with fur, fought through snow. And the seasons tumbled, and he walked and walked. In a clearing of birdsong he stopped and looked all around. The wind had gone and it was still; the only sound was the chatter of water in a stream, full of the winter melting. And the man looked at the stream and remembered he was thirsty; he crouched down in the soft moss and cupped his hands and closed his eyes. The hair on the back of his hands was a pale fine down, and the silver water from the stream ran not through the tangle of a beard but over fair skin. His eyes changed from dark brown to blue, and when he was done drinking he stood tall in the clearing, and it was summer, and an axe was in his hand. It was the one he had inherited from his father – the most precious thing he possessed.

And he decided that here he would build his farm, that this was a good place. The hills encircled him, protected the place from the worst of the west winds, and there was water – sweet and pure. He had no neighbours and on that day at the beginning of summer he wanted none; he had come seeking solitude and that was all he had found. He began work with the axe, and in the good summer days with their long light he cut his wood and shaped it. All night he slept under the stars and was troubled by nothing but dreams of the place he had left behind. But he shrugged them away when he wakened once more, went down to where the stream fell into the blue eye of a lochan, deep and sore with cold, and swam there, naked, until he was himself.

That first house was finished on Christmas Eve, and he called it the House of the Sparrow – for a sparrow followed him for crumbs all November as the sleet came sideways on the wind. It was also because the house was barely more than a shelter, a place in which to stay alive through the rock and howl of winter. For a fever gripped him not five days after the House of the Sparrow was finished, a fever through which he heard shouting and old anger rekindled. And when he rose up in his sleep, his naked back a shining sea of sweat, there was nothing but the whine of the wind in the darkness, and the wet snow pattering on the door.

Starve a fever. Aye, he starved two whole weeks, only drinking and drinking the sweet water that came from the burn outside. And one morning he woke up on his back and was dry, and there was a single bird singing, its voice clear and strong and rich, and it felt as though he had been washed through some vast ocean, tumbled and broken in it, and left at last on the deserted white sand of a beach.

He got up, his head light and full of air, and opened the door. The cold met him and the hills glistened with ice; he stood there shivering, and a robin fluttered down and landed in the bowl of his open left hand, and he smiled. It was spring.

He knew he was lonely the morning he heard the first

cuckoo. He was up in the wood on the hunt for boulders to build a new wall when he heard it. Very far away beyond him, muffled and almost lost in the wood. But he stood tall and his first thought was to tell someone. His mouth opened and the words fell to dust, for who was there to tell? As a boy he had always come running home with news of the first cuckoo. It had been a thing of luck; the promise of blue days and new beginnings.

That night he lay in the House of the Sparrow and heard the silence for the first time. He heard it and did not know what to do with it. There was a soreness in his chest and he turned over and over in search of something he could not find. The morning came up in red gashes and he thudded down to swim, but he could not wash away what wronged him.

He dressed and walked down the glen for the first time. He followed the river that led him, that bounced joyous before him like a wild puppy, gathering new burns all the while, becoming wide and strong-shouldered as it went.

And he came to a bridge over the river. It was something the like of which he had not seen for a long time, and he marvelled at the magic of it, that it arched in a bow with nothing to hold it – all those thousands of stones. And he was so deep in wondering and watching he never saw two young lads behind him, and as they passed they laughed at him with toothless mouths, and the one spat and after he had spat he spoke: 'That'll be the gouk that lives up in the wood!'

And it was as if those two voices woke others in his head, for over the bridge were houses and smoke and other roads. He went over and found himself amidst braying and bleating, for it was market day and the thick stink of sharn was in the air. There were women too, with aprons and headscarves, laughing and talking and jigging each other's elbows, and he tried not to stare at the blue jewels of their eyes and the buttery sheen of their faces. For he remembered he was bashed and ugly from his months of labour on the house, and he had not cared then but he cared now. He shrank into a doorway and watched a man playing with fire and a dog catching rings of wood, and the young girls stood watching, and the thoughts rumbled in his head like thunder, and the heat grew in his great hands.

'Will you have a glass of beer?'

He whirled round and saw a girl in the shadows, tight gold ringlets on her forehead and her face small and shy. He felt for the words in his throat for it was long, long since he last spoke, and his heart hammered his chest and fought to be still. He stumbled to a seat, half-seeing men in the shadows around him, and somehow the words formed and his voice softened, and the girl who had brought him in spoke with him. She filled other glasses and flashed smiles at other men and took their coins, but always she came back to him, stood and listened and talked. And as he drank he became himself and told her about the cuckoo he had heard that morning. He told her about the House of the Sparrow and the creatures he had seen in the glen. And she filled his glass again and there was fiddle music in his ears, and his heart flamed for the golden ringlets on her forehead, and he talked until he had no more to say. He got up, and the dark room with its smoke and voices swam around him, and she dried a glass with a white cloth.

'You never told me your name!'

'Somerled,' he said, and felt the shyness fill him once more.

'Somerled,' she said, and it was different on her tongue. It was like a glade full of sunlight and bees, warm and beautiful. She said his name and it laughed in her mouth, and she said it again and again.

'It's a name I never heard before,' she said. 'My name's just Anna.'

And he wanted to say it was fine, that it was as fine as she was, but his courage had gone and he was himself, awkward and battered after his labours, a nobody from up the glen. And he saw in his mind's eye the toothless lads on the bridge. So he said nothing but stood, a boy, shy, cap in scuffed hands.

She leaned on the dark wood of the bar, the glass curled in her hand.

'You never paid for your beer,' she said, but not angry, her voice kind enough. 'You can pay me with a visit to the House of the Sparrow, so come back and find me.'

Then she was gone and he was pushed through the sweat and noise and laughter into the bright world beyond. And he fell over a dog and as he rose and went the laughter came like nails down his back and his face burned with shame. He felt sick for he had drunk too fast and hadn't let beer pass his lips since the day he left home. A sourness filled his head and a drum thudded at his temples, and the late sun was sore in his eyes as he trudged the miles home.

And the following day Anna was like the barest threads of a dream, something he had wished, had dared might happen and was passed now, was gone. He went on with his wall, his mouth dry and his head heavy, a sad weight dull in his heart.

For days he was no different and his wall was a feeble huddle of rocks. He was good for nothing and he sat, hunched forward, and he thought. And he heard the last words she had uttered soft and kind in the cave of his head. They echoed and sang, and he knew that his hands would be useless till he'd gone back there. For all that he thought and ate and slept was called Anna.

This time he dusted his clothes and tied back his hair. He washed his face in the burning cold of the lochan, and when the water had stilled once more he stared long at himself to be sure he was ready to meet her once more. He walked the miles and heard the hammer of his heart. He thought of his words and tugged them around and listened to them in the still air, for every one had to be good. And he heard the cuckoo above him in the glen and took it like a good omen, put it in his pocket like a charm. And when he went into the inn three men turned round, their eyes sour and yellow, and two were the lads he'd met on the bridge.

'A funny smell in here today,' said the one, looking right at him.

'Aye, it's strong all right,' said the other. 'Must be shite from up the glen. I reckon the wind's got up and blown the stink all the way down here.'

Somerled stopped and he saw Anna hovering at the back of the bar. But he was riled by their rudeness; he had met this kind of talk before and he wasn't about to turn tail. And there was a spark too that wanted to light for Anna, though maybe it was buried so deep he hardly knew it was there himself.

'You won't smell it if you go outside.'

The two lads crawled from their stools and the stink of their mouths and unshaven faces went before them. Like beasts they slouched to the door, and when the second had shouldered his way out, Somerled slipped to his side, caught the two by their collars and dunted their heads together like coconuts. They went down sprawling, clutching at the sides of their heads and wailing. The third man sat on at the bar as Somerled slipped back in.

'Come on, Anna – let's go!'

And they went, running and laughing and falling over their own feet for laughter. They talked over each other and their hands brushed together and the sunlight came like coins on the river, and there was the bar of an eagle over one of the bens. And Somerled felt as though he had made it himself, as though all of this was his own, and he dared to catch her hand and she was happy.

He showed her where the owl fluttered among the trees at dusk, and he took her up to see the view over the hills, the highest of them tipped with the last grey snow. They came back to the House of the Sparrow as a hailstorm broke over the glen, and together they watched at the window as the ground turned to a white slush and the hills were lost under thunderheads of cloud.

'I like it here,' she whispered, and he heard the smile in her voice.

And he wanted to ask her even then, but the courage fled as he turned, and he knew in his heart it was madness. They had known each other one day, and a day was the blink of an eye.

'Will you come and see where I live?' she asked, her voice shy, not daring to turn to look.

And he pulled her round, made her look. 'Of course I will!' he said, as though it was strange she even asked.

'You know those boys in the bar?' she said, still not looking.

'Yes . . .'

'They're my brothers!'

And the two of them laughed till the tears coursed down their cheeks. They laughed till they rolled on the wood of the floor he had made and their faces met and they kissed. And the hail was gone and a great hayfield of sunlight burned through the glen.

'I'd better be nice to them the next time I see them,' he breathed, and they kissed again, this time deep and true and long.

'You can walk me home,' she said, and struggled up, and he didn't want her to go, and he thought how it would be if she were there in the darkness of the House of the Sparrow. And his hands were clumsy with her things and she laughed at him and ruffled his fine blond hair.

And they didn't walk, they ran. For her father would be angry if she were to be late home, she cried, and Somerled tried to catch up with her as she ran down the track. All the way to the village she ran and Somerled at her back, the bang of his heart in his head. And over the bridge, slow, his legs like lead, breathless, still following Anna as best he could. And she led him to the blacksmith's yard, and a man looked up from the hoof he was holding, a man big as a bear, but the smile that crossed his face was gentle as a child's, and his eyes danced in the fur of a black beard and tangle of black curls.

'So you've met Anna then?'

And what could he do but nod? It sounded final, as though

that was that, and in a sense it was true, for he would have been glad if Anna had packed up her things that night and come back to the house for ever. But Anna took his useless hand as he stood there and led him back to her house. And who should they meet in the doorway but the boys whose heads he had cracked together like rocks. And now like sheepdogs they slunk about, their heads down, and Somerled said something he hardly understood himself and held out his hand, and they shook it as though it was a cabbage leaf and shuffled away to be anywhere else but there.

In the kitchen a small, plump woman turned round from the stove and her face was a whole smile. She babbled about onions and meat, and half of it Somerled never heard, but he nodded and was happy, was happy there with Anna gold at his side. And he met dogs and cats and an old woman who lived in the house too but didn't seem to belong to anyone. And then they ate at the table after grace, everyone talking and asking him questions. Only the boys sat together, hunched over their bowls and grim. He felt tired when all of it was over, tired but good, as Anna kissed him goodnight and he padded home through the warm blue shadows of the dusk. The trees were windless and the hills stood round him in the glen like dark shields. The air was full of moths and the river sang its own song, over and over. He came home and closed the door and lay down to sleep, but the day spun through his head with its strangeness. It felt as though he flew and it took hours and hours to land once more and come back to himself.

But the next day he rose with new purpose, for the House of the Sparrow was nothing but a shelter. He worked like one possessed, preparing wood and bringing boulders, for what he wanted would be a melding of wood and rock. He went back and forth to the village, for he needed nails and glass and tools, and all manner of things he had never used before. And when the rowans hung in blood orange clusters and the first winds rose with autumn, Somerled was almost done. Exhausted, he slept on the floor of his own house for two whole days, his hands clasped under him, blue and bashed and sore. He woke to the wind rising around the house, and he looked down into the glen and saw the backs of the red deer as they roamed, the stags that were full of the blood of autumn. And something rose within him too; something ancient and magnificent filled him, as sap fills a living tree, and he felt a great strength lift him that became also a great joy. He was ready; he was ready at last.

He walked the track to the village seeing everything: the hints of amethyst and dark yellow and bright orange that lighted here and here and here in the glen. He heard the long echoes of the stags' roars from the hillsides, and he felt a gladness that this was the place where he was to be. He had chosen it without thought and it had been right. He might live three times over and want no more than this place and this glen. Like that he came over the bridge into the village and wondered that there was no one about. Deserted it was; nothing but the swallows and martins looping the still air, and he gave a call and there was no answer, just a door banging in the edge of a breeze that lifted the trees.

And he came past the church and looked at its dark walls and unstained windows, and from inside came the lift and fall of song. Like the saltwater of the sea it was; great waves of song that carried the heart and opened it completely. And

Somerled dragged the tangle of hat from his head and stood bowed, for he knew that someone was being mourned. And he waited until they came out in black straggles, the wind now in hair and scarves; he waited until he saw Allan Campbell, Anna's father, coming over the grass towards him. And the tears stood in the eyes of that great bear of a man, and he had no shame for them, nor did he try to wipe them away.

'Ah, Joseph was a good man! He was blessed with ninety good years on this earth and he'll be missed for many more.'

And he put his great arm around Somerled and smiled through his tears.

'But I bet it's Anna you're here to find! She'll be getting ready at the inn, for every man and dog will be there to drink by the time it's dark. Not the best day you could have chosen, my boy!'

Somerled nodded and smiled and rolled his eyes and thanked him. He went there all the same and waited in a corner, nursing a dark glass one, two and three hours. But he watched her content, a glow of warmth in him for he knew that from the first she had given herself to him and would be his. There was talk all around him and gusts of laughter, but he sat in his own dreams, content with quiet.

And one by one they went in the end, and with them their whistles and fiddles and songs, and he crept soft out of the shadows so she gave a start. And her face filled with a summer of smiles.

'Somerled Stewart! I might have known. Were you there the whole time and said nothing? Wait until I get my coat!'

Outside the night were stars, a full frost of them over the

11

northern sky. And there were lights in all the houses the colour of lemon.

'I came because the house is done,' he explained, happy and shy.

And she reached up and kissed him a single time, soft as a snowflake. 'Show me then,' she said, impatient.

'Are you not too tired?'

'Not to see this!'

So they ran there under the starlight, and the glen was as bright as day. Then, madly, he swept her up into his arms and carried her the whole way up to the house as she shrieked and laughed and wriggled.

And inside she marvelled at things that made him pleased. For he had done this for her and no one else. And the rooms were full of silver light that made everything strange and beautiful. And he followed her, a little behind all the time, watching her, happy.

Then they walked back, slow and easy, the quiet between them good, the moon a bowl of silver to the east of them. And they came to the bridge and she stopped.

'So when are we getting married? Everyone's asking, and I'd want it before winter. I've waited long enough and you won't tell me.'

But his white face and half-open mouth could only make her laugh.

'Somerled Stewart, you look like a stuffed trout! I didn't mean to scare you and you can have all the time you need. But I do love you.'

And she stroked back the pale down of hair at his forehead and held the one hand cupped around his cheek as she kissed him, slow and tender. Then her name was called into the night, half-worried, and it was her mother, and she answered as she ran over the bridge, waving and smiling to Somerled who still hadn't said a word.

The night washed back, beautiful, with just the first edge of autumn. His father had used to say there was a knife on the edge of the night, meaning that there would be a frost. He walked home slow and thoughtful, knowing that Anna was right, but thinking not so much of when they would be married but more what they would live from.

The next day was his own; there was nothing to be hammered or measured or smoothed. A scatter of rain came over at eight, and all of it pattered on the roof. He held his breath as though afraid it might come in.

He resolved to go up to the high loch. The day was torn between gloom and fierce sunlight. He went fast, up through a giants' chessboard of rocks beyond the wood, and then onto the moorland proper. The bell heather was the colour of amethyst, tall sometimes as his shoulders. He fought his way on, searching for a path he never found, climbing and climbing all the time. And in the sun's fire he grew hot and yearned to drink, but there was nothing in the burns but a flicker of silver, for the summer had been long and dry.

And then he came to a clearing, a place of more rocks and a thin blue water. And all around there were things growing he had never seen before. Beaded berries they were, small as the nail of his pinkie, some orange and some almost white. He crouched and gathered them, smelling the sweetness of them, and his mouth filled with a yellow sweetness, a honeyed loveliness that made him search in the hope of more. And he thought of the Children of Israel as they trudged across the wilderness, and he reckoned this had been a kind of manna too.

So he went on again, but now he had reached a plateau, and he could see the loch set in the heather ahead of him like a sky-blue gem in a brooch. He swam through the deep heather, a whole hour and more, his legs heavy and hurting, until he was there on the shore at last. And out on the water was an island of rowans and birch and willow, and as he crouched down on the tiny beach of red-gold sand, he wondered if any soul had stood on that island in the long story of the world.

For he had heard tales of the early people in Scotland who had chosen islets as places of safety. And when the Celts came they had thought such places sacred; they had thought all islands set apart and precious. And it came to him that the place he had found in the glen was set apart and special too; he had found it but it had been a gift, and in a way it was a kind of island as this was. And there and then he resolved that when he and Anna made it their home it would be such a crannog, a place set apart, an island. They would not forget that, or, if they did, they would remember what it was to be and return in their hearts to find and restore it.

And he lay back and listened to the whisper of the wind in the grass and the heather, and he heard the mourning of birds in the sky, long and beautiful was their crying. And he watched the blue-white changing of the sky above him, and he knew that whatever was to happen he would love this place and call it home. For the old nightmares he had come with, in the days when he first built the House of the Sparrow, they did not plague him any longer. They were part of another world, a world he had left behind him.

He got up and drank, and washed his face in the pure blue cold of the loch. And he remembered why he had come. What was he going to do to live? He saw the black reflection of his head and shoulders in the ruffling water and he wondered. He had chosen his place in the glen and for that reason he had no wish to spend his days somewhere in the village. There would be enough coming and going to the place without that. He looked down and saw his wet hands, still red and raw from their weeks of labour on the house. He had learned much, that was true, but he had been born with good hands too. He could find things in wood; he could see things that were there and bring them out.

For the first time he noticed pieces of wood up at the top of the tiny beach. They were ghosts of wood, ancient and gnarled and hard as mountains. Yet as he turned one he saw a wren sleeping there. And in the other might be a stag, its head lifting and roaring its autumn hunger. Or was he only imagining? They might lie there, but was he ready to find them? Had he hands that good?

There was only one way to find out. He turned and looked at the island a last time, and the light that fell over the loch was a melding of red and blue and gold. Then he began the long road back, and it seemed further than before, and he fought through the heather and felt half-dead before he came to the place where he had found the berries. He felt the sweat pour from him as he plunged down towards the house, the house that was hidden still among the trees.

When at last he was back, the flies circling his head and

his face flushed and scratched, he dropped the two pieces of wood by the door and went down to the lochan to swim. He poured himself into the water where it was deepest, and he made rings as he circled and plunged, and the cool healed the burning of his head.

Up then he went and swept the dark knotted wood into his hand. He was about to open the door of the house when he stopped. He looked up to the crown of the hill and the House of the Sparrow. What if it was there he was to work? Why not there?

He found his tools and his hands shook. He strode up to the first place he had made, hardly able to reach it quickly enough, and he opened the door. It was dry and bright, and it had the quiet he needed to think. For he knew he must have quiet about him or nothing at all could be found.

But he was frightened to begin. He went away to eat because he was hungry; he set the fire in the grate, he mended a windowframe. And all the time his tools and the two pieces of wood burned in his mind and waited for him, and at last he swore, foolishly and uselessly, and he thudded back up to the House of the Sparrow. And he began. He was less frightened of finding the wren – that would be the easier of the two – and that was the one he started.

Even he was taken aback by the hardness of that wood. It was like working with stone. Twice he cut himself and the bright blood shone on his pale hands. But he kept on, digging and digging until he was ready to start finding the bird. And now his hands trembled again, but it was because he was on fire, something that had been set alight inside and he knew what the knife must do, what it must do now and what it must do next. It came to him, it was there inside, and the wren grew – wings and tail and beak – and it was the same wren that was there round the house in the spring.

When he was done he looked up. Out of the window he saw the clear white skies of evening and the chink of a single star. There wasn't a breath of wind and he had not a clue what time it must be – he had lost all sense of time completely. And it did not matter.

And his first thought when he finished was that he wished Anna could see what he had made. But his second was that he knew what he wanted to do in the future, for his hands were ready.

There was a morning he knew it was autumn. He got up, slow and heavy, and he moved as through deep water. But something had come to him in a dream, something he remembered from a long time ago, and it had given him an idea. It was also something that lay within his hands. And when he was ready at last he went out into the wild reds and thrashing golds of the morning. The wind chased from everywhere at once, and the hillsides came and went in a swirling of mist. And when Somerled turned once to walk backwards a moment, his raw hands buried in his pockets, he saw the glinting of quartz on the highest hills. The wolves of winter were coming closer. He had no time to lose.

He went into the inn and there were a few old men at a table. Men who had worked their years with sheep or in the fields, who were married now to the bottle. And Anna's face shone like a sunrise when she saw him: she leaned her arms tight on the dark wood of the bar so her breasts pressed close and hard, and there was talk and the murmur of laughter about them, but neither of them heard a thing.

'I've an answer to your question,' he said gently, sitting to one side on the tall stool at the end of the bar. 'We can be married when the gift I'm making you is finished.'

Anna shone pink with joy and curiosity and confusion. She liked what he had said, but the words of an answer tumbled about in her head, and one didn't know which would go in front of the other.

Then he was off again, leaving her in a whirlwind. And he liked that himself, and the fact that she half-called his name as he went through the door and that he didn't turn round. The first brown curls of leaves scurried about the street and he went in to see the jeweller, and the old fellow got up and shook him by the hand and bade him have a seat. And Somerled explained what he intended to do, and the jeweller, Angus Grant, put his elbows on the table and listened and nodded and thought it was possible and would do it if he could. And that was it. Somerled went in to see Martha, his mother-in-law to be, and of course there was tea and a scone and talk. Talk about foxes and farms and news of war on the other side of the world, but he knew that what she really wanted to know was when the big day would be.

'I'm making a gift for Anna,' he said, his head bent and his eyes on the table. 'And when that's done . . .'

So all that remained now was to *make* the gift, but he had not the faintest idea how long that would take.

He had been told of a place up the river, up at the bottleneck of the glen. And by the time he went there, to a loneliness that seemed beyond the world, the river came down in a roar of silver so the loudest shouting would have drowned in it. He stood there a time, under it, and felt the roaring of the earth beneath his feet and blinked. Small he was, small beneath this might. But then at last he remembered himself and awoke, as though from a dream, and the words he had been told by the man in the inn came back to him: *Look for a beach up to the left of the fall. That's the place for finding, but it's a secret, mind, and it's a gift I'm giving you!*

He picked up the cloth bag he'd brought and looked out across the boiling pools, shining like polished cairngorm. There was no way across, and he was no strong swimmer. His eyes danced about, and thirty yards downstream he spied a place where jagged rocks stuck up to make a crossing. One or two waggled like loose teeth as he teetered his way across, but he leaped from the last one and his feet drove into the shingle. And so he stood beside the lions of the falls and felt the spit of the spray on his face. Up and up he scrambled until he came to the little beach the man had surely spoken of, and his whole heart hammered in his chest. He opened his cloth bag and brought out first a spade; not a thing a man might have to dig with, but rather built for a child – something to crouch with and spoon away the earth. He took care where he began and dug away the thick silt slow and easy, deep until he had scraped the bedrock. It was the very deepest stuff he brought to the surface, and it was this he tipped careful into a small copper pan. He dropped the spade and, kneeling at the pool's edge, dipped it in the dark water. He swirled it and swirled it so sparkles of light danced up and were gone.

That first time everything washed away in the end. Perhaps he felt a kind of foolish disappointment at that, as though he had expected it to work like magic. But he had to learn too; his hands knew all about wood, and they'd grown used enough to great rocks – but what did he know of little stones? He looked up and realised he was half-soaked from the spray of the falls already. When you looked from there, crouched on that tiny shingle shore, it was as though the kettle-drums of the fall would sweep you away, swirl you into their cauldrons for ever. And for a moment, as he crouched there, he imagined an early man having found the place and watching, believing that this must be the very home of the gods.

He bent down once more and tried to dig deeper still; his spade scraped the ledge on which the boulder above rested. Even so, he brought up a thin layer of silt and let it fall, careful, in the pan. It seemed hardly enough to take the trouble over, and he was about to dig once more, when he shrugged his shoulders and let it be. A little water ran in over the edge of the pan, and slow and steady he swirled, careful, his eyes wide and watching.

And there, right away, was something that shone out at him from the washed layer of silt. His thumb and forefinger scrabbled madly to take hold of it, for it was big. A lump of yellow with dents and bumps as he turned it round in the light, and he threw his head back and laughed aloud, for he had begun! He scrabbled about in the bag and found a little leather bag, and with all the care in the world he opened the drawstrings and dropped it inside.

Then he hunted like a creature possessed – for an hour or two hours or more. And there was nothing. Sparkles that floated away; fool's gold and mica that glinted and mocked him. And he was soaked through and felt a fool, felt all of this had been madness, nothing more than a wild goose chase. He left the beach and went back the way he had come, scrabbled his way over the boulders and came to the other side. He had seen another gold; the bright white gold of the late sun on the other side of the glen. And he came out of the shadows into its glory, and he found a place to lie, stretched on his back, and looked again at the one nugget of gold, and remembered it was at least a beginning.

Before he started home that evening he found two more pieces of what might have been gold. One, he feared, was wishful thinking – the other was more likely. He twirled them endlessly in the candlelight, and they were beautiful things – they had been worth every moment of the search. But how long would this take; how long did he have?

For the next days he felt a kind of prisoner of the place. He trailed there through the steel thrashing of rain, and swirled and swirled until his hands were sore with cold. He was near weeping with it, with the madness of this, for a task that might never be completed. And all that time he never went near the village but was hidden away in his house, wondering and worrying. For there was never anything the size of that first bit of gold. He found flashes, things he was sure were real enough, but they were little more than dustings. His hands and heart were weary; he grew afraid he might have to admit defeat.

And that in turn made him lie awake in the night and wonder. Was that what he was, one who could never be beaten, who had to win? For it made him remember the shadow of home and all he had left to forget. And figures flickered through his dreams, and spoke words to him that lay deep within his memory, as deep as the gold in the beach under the great falls.

But he went back all the same, unslept and white and gaunt. He went back and stood under the great horses of water that galloped down into the pools below and were gone, as though asking that this might yet happen as he had dreamed it might. It was a day of strangeness; a silver light played and went in the skies, and there was a stillness, and two ravens floated beyond the glen and were lost in unknown skies. But as he looked back at the river and the falls, Somerled saw something he had not seen before. It was a tiny fragment of shingle ten and more feet higher than where he had been for all these days. It was all but hidden between great dark spars of rock, and he did not know if he could reach it. Yet it came to him that perhaps it was this beach of which the old man had spoken, that it was there the real treasure lay. And he moved upwards with care, afraid that in his eagerness he might fall and split his skull on the rocks below. Slow and slow, hand over hand, up until his hand touched the ledge where it was hidden. A whole half-hour it took him to get there, and there was hardly room to move once he crouched between the dark guardian stones. But he was there and he began just the same.

And the gold came. Nothing as big as that first piece, but little bits of shining grit nonetheless. He had no thought of how long he remained there; he neither ate nor drank nor once stopped for rest. But when he was done a trickle of golden fragments sang as he poured them from his hand safe into the leather bag.

And somehow he knew that he was done, and that the little ledge had no more gold to yield. And he walked home, half-crippled after crouching all those hours, and he lit a fire, and ate and drank his fill, and slept dreamless until well into the next day.

But as soon as he was awake he remembered. He dressed well, took his pouch and put it safe in his canvas bag, and hobbled down the glen to the village. He felt strange and raw among folk; he had spoken to no one for six long days.

'Well, you're fairly looking the weary one, Somerled Stewart! Don't tell me Anna's got you cleaning and polishing already!'

He laughed all right at the postman's words as he whirred past on his cycle, but he could think of no words of reply. His head was empty. He hoped he would make no fool of himself in front of Angus Grant. But the man was gentle, brought him to a seat and said nothing but what a fine autumn day it was. And he had been wondering how Somerled's hunt had been going.

And Somerled said nothing but poured out the fine trail of gold onto a piece of black velvet that Angus put down on the table. And there at the edge was the one big nugget.

'Well, you've done well indeed,' said Angus, his head bent over the little heap of treasure, as he poked it with tiny tweezers.

'But is it enough?' Somerled asked. 'Will it be sufficient for a ring?'

Angus Grant lifted his head and smiled.

'I'll make you a ring of it all right. It'll be thin, mind, but it'll be enough!'

So Somerled left and above him in the street, the trees shimmered with the golden morning light. He wanted to run and tell Anna, and it was the one thing he couldn't do. But he went instead and hammered at the minister's door, and suddenly he was so full of the joy of talk he couldn't stop babbling. And even the minister, usually grey and quiet and full of his own thoughts, leaned forward and touched the wrist of his right hand, the curl of a smile on his lips.

'I have time to talk, Somerled. I'm catching no lunchtime train!'

And he knew then he was being foolish, but it didn't matter. They decided on the last day of October, and Somerled said as he was leaving he just prayed it wouldn't rain. And he could have bitten off his tongue for that, but it was said and nothing for it. He went to see about clothes and shoes and this thing and that, and he wondered still if he should see Anna, and hung a time about the door of the inn like a lost dog. But he knew he'd only blurt out the whole story if he did see her, and what was the point of all the secrecy if it was over like that?

But he couldn't resist going in to see Martha all the same. She hugged him and he was well-nigh smothered by her, so happy she was to see him after all these long days.

'And here was me thinking you'd got cold feet and had gone running off back to the west! But you're thin, Somerled Stewart. I couldn't see you if you stood sideways! Now, no arguments and you're staying for your dinner. It's no matter whether there's six or seven at the table. You'll not see Anna for she'll have hers at the inn, but here come Euan and Iain because they've smelled the soup, and if I know Allan he'll hardly be far behind! Euan, would you call Mary, and you've coal dust all over your face!'

So he became himself again in their midst, and Euan even sat beside him that day and told him about a pine marten they were after – the rascal had been seen by the church several times now. And Somerled asked with a straight face if that meant it was likely it was a religious pine marten, and Allan heard the tail end of it too, and they rolled their eyes and laughed, and the whole table had to hear the story. It was good to be among them, to feel he was part of a family once more, and he thought of his own and wondered what it would be like to go into that kitchen unannounced one day. And he saw his mother's face turning pale to his own as he came in . . .

'Somerled! Can you hear us? We're asking about the big day; if you're any closer to knowing when it's to be?'

And he heard them at last and looked at them sheepish and told them, said that had been the main reason for coming, and Martha said she wouldn't sleep until it was over there was so much to be done. But they were happy and that was enough. And he slipped away in the midst of their happiness, for suddenly he wanted to be back, on his own. It was as though he felt something coming alive in his hands; a kind of twitching. And he didn't run but he might have done; he came into the house breathless as the whole glen bloomed in the dusk.

He searched half-mad for a piece of wood, for anything at all, and there was just a knuckle-end of a piece he found in the House of the Sparrow. But that was enough, for suddenly he had seen a mouse sleeping in that bit of wood and it wanted finding.

And to his own surprise it was done fast and he turned it

in his left hand when it was ready, and a warm well of delight burst somewhere inside him. All afternoon he came back to look at it and pick it up, and he tried not to be proud, but was it wrong to be glad for something your own hands had made well?

And two days before the month's end and the beginning of a new world, he grew afraid. It came over him as he stood at the side window and saw the snow that crowned the corries and bens before him. What if all of this was as the butterflies of summer? The lure of a moment's sunlight before the clouds come and sweep it away for ever. Ten years lay between Anna and him, and what if they were ten years too many? Suddenly, as though taken right out of himself, he stood in the sea room of the house where he had grown up, and he was a child again. But his mother was as he last knew her, her face turned hard and the blue of her eyes gone to stone, and her lips thin and pressed tight. She looked right at him, and he felt again the fear he had once known.

Love is not about the bright days of summer. That is the delusion, the web that has tangled so many. Love is about the dark days, the days of storm, the days when there is no power. Most only learn that too late and suffer the lesson they have to learn. But there is another way . . .

Somerled came back to himself, dizzy, steadied himself against the windowframe. There was a gentle tapping on the door outside and he heard his name being called. He reckoned the postman must have knocked before.

'Sorry, Lachie, in another world! Just leave them and be on your way!'

But the postman was still leaning round the door, beaming.

'Ah, you won't know what's hit you by the end of the week, Somerled, boy! There'll be no time to stand and stare, I can tell you!'

Then the laughter swept from his face and he looked at Somerled gentle, kind. His own wife had died five years past, and why they never found out.

'Have a grand day and make the most of it. And here's to all that lies ahead.'

When the postman had turned away and started down the track, Somerled went back to the window where he had stood before. Perhaps there was something of him that wanted to find the door back to the childhood room and the words of his mother. He had felt himself there for however long it lasted, and somehow he sensed she had not finished speaking. But there was nothing, just a late autumn fly buzzing against the windowpane. He lifted the palm of his hand to kill it, without thinking, and then stopped. What would his days of light be in the great span of eternity? He creaked open the window and let the fly out into the last sunlight of autumn.

There were just two envelopes, and one was another bill. He would have to begin carving in earnest, and making a name for himself, if they were to live here and think of bringing a family into the world. But the other had writing that was oddly familiar to him. It wasn't addressed to the house in the glen, but to the post office in the village. He held it a long time, sure he knew whose writing it must be, and not remembering. But then he shook his head, as though admitting defeat, and tore the envelope open.

Dear Somerled

It's strange to write to you now, after all this time, and I don't even know if my letter will reach you. I do think of you often, and I heard from someone who travels to the corner where you've settled that you've built a house and are to be married. I'm glad for you.

Do you know, when I think back to childhood (and it's not something I have the courage to do very often), I think of being in that room at the front of the house, the one we used to call the sea room. Do you remember playing there for hours? We were never supposed to make it dirty, because it was for guests and our dear mother knew how to put fear into us of that. But we still brought in crabs and sea urchins and all manner of other things.

Dear Somerled, I need to run quickly and catch the post before it's too late, but the good news is that I want to be and can be at your wedding! I'm overjoyed, and I can't wait to meet your bride.

Be well until then, and with my love,

Deirdre

He read it through three times, his hands trembling. His sister Deirdre! But what almost unnerved him with its strangeness was that at the very moment the letter arrived with its talk of the sea room, he had been there himself in some extraordinary way. And he hadn't thought of the place for years!

He realised that the piece of paper carried no address; he had no idea how he would reply. Did she not want him to know where she was, or had she written in such haste there had been no time? He was all but certain it must be the former, and that made him wonder why. Was she ashamed or afraid? He thought of how beautiful she had been as a child, of how he had felt when visitors came to the house and bent down to touch her golden curls. He remembered how his heart had actually felt sore, how he had gone away to hide because Deirdre was better than him! They never said anything about his gold head, or about his blue eyes! Nor did they bother to come to find him, to hug him and bend down and tell him that he was special too. They left him upstairs, waiting, until the tears that streaked down his face had dried. He came down, into the dining room, and was given a row for being late.

But she was right all the same – they had played in the sea room! He remembered one summer evening, when neither of them could sleep for the warm stillness, when they crept downstairs and out. They padded down to the beach in bare feet, and the sea was miles out – they could see it, a chalk line so far away, but they could hear the rush and hiss of it still. And it was the one time they found starfish, living starfish. He remembered his starfish being big, but that was most likely because of the smallness of his hands. The two of them forgot themselves completely, and shrieked and laughed as they played, and carried back three living starfish, and breathless came back and into the porch.

'And what the devil do you think you've been doing?'

He remembered seeing his mother's boots first. His eyes rose, from her boots to her skirt, to the white cardigan she wore in the evenings, to her folded arms and the blue stone of her eyes. He dropped the bucket of starfish and saw his wet, sand-spattered legs.

What was worst was that she did not raise her voice. It was all spoken low and bloodless and utterly cold, and now they heard their father too, somewhere upstairs, calling and asking what was going on. He came, tying his dressing gown, his own feet bare.

'Oh, Deirdre, and you know you have the party tomorrow morning! You'll catch a stinker of a cold! You are silly, and, yes, I know it's warm, but it makes no difference. I expect it was all Somerled's idea, wasn't it? We'll have a bath – yes, no arguments, because tomorrow we'll all be in a rush!'

Somerled looked down at the letter, and the sea and the house and his childhood fell back into it and were gone. He heard the clock strike ten. Yes, it would be good to see Deirdre. He was glad she was coming.

And two days later the wind rose as though it too would be a guest at the wedding. It rushed through the trees and the hillsides shone in quick blinks of light. His hand was shaken thirty times, even by old Bobo, who hadn't known what day of the year it was since the end of the last war. And Colonel James, he came to shake hands, he and Lady Moira. They were sorry they couldn't be at the service, but Lady Moira had lost a brother in Helensburgh and they were off south today.

And then someone was hurrying him and patting the hair down on his head and telling him something he never properly heard. He drifted into the church and there was a sea of faces, and he tried to look ahead for fear of falling. And then the minister was telling him it was all right and he looked fine, and the best man came in a hurry (he had been held up by a lost sheep). Roddy, who he didn't know, and who sometimes had terrible fights with bottles of whisky, but apart from that was as dependable as a rock. And he looked all round for Deirdre and ached to see her, but there was no sign, and he wondered wildly if perhaps she had changed her mind. And there was a soreness in his heart at that, for no one from his family was there at all, and it would have meant something . . .

But then Anna came on the arm of her father and their eyes met, and a warmth filled the whole of him and all but took away his breath. For she outshone everything; the light of her and something that beat in her he had known in no one else. And he remembered that market day he had come into the village, shy and foolish, and how she had chosen him even then for her own. And the words that the minister read from the Bible about love were beautiful; he forced his heart to slow to hear them, for he remembered the stern words of his mother as he had heard her so strangely two days before. And somehow they held together and he knew that with all his soul he would fight to keep this, not to let the darkness eat it away and destroy it.

And before he knew it the ring was on Anna's finger, and he had yet to tell her its story. They were out into the white rush of the sunlight, and he froze yet he laughed and was swept along to the hall. And he had been told not to put a foot in that direction, and he kissed Martha for her kindness and pumped Allan's arm. There was dancing and songs and enough food to keep a small country content for a fortnight. And Roddy, who had been sober a long while (though not, perhaps, quite as long as he thought) sought the company of Kirsty from over the hill and began to make a good dent in the whisky barrel. But when Somerled was back in the shadows, and on his own for a moment, and wondering which child had been left out of a dance, something touched the edge of his sleeve and he looked around, startled.

Half the face was gone, as though melted, and he searched the other half unsure, yet knowing somehow all the same.

'It's me, Somerled,' said the face. 'It's me, Deirdre.'

And he knew, and held her close, and cried even though it was his wedding day. He cried because it was her and he cried for everything else, for all that had been left behind and unburied.

'But what happened?' he demanded, his eye drifting to the side of her face that was gone. For she was his sister, and he could ask.

'Not now,' she said, shaking her head, but her voice soft. 'One day I'll tell you and we'll talk; perhaps we can even go back and make our peace, but not tonight. I'm just glad for you.'

And he held her again, and all at once Anna was there, calling for him to come with her. But with pride he presented Deirdre, as though he had magicked her out of the air himself. And as Anna smiled and said she had to drag him away he turned round and asked Deirdre where she had come from to be there, but her words were swallowed by the noise and he was gone.

And the night had almost passed when Allan and Martha clapped their hands and slowly the talk and the laughter and the music faded.

'Time to take them home!' they called, and from nowhere seemed to come great bunches of rowan with their full clutches. Outside, in the silver-white of the night began a procession, silent but glad. And at the front were Allan and Martha, leading the way, and at the back came Somerled and Anna, their hands clasped. And the rowan branches were held aloft at the sides of the procession, and they formed a sacred wood, a protective and ancient forest, almost as though it was a kind of promise, to protect and love through all that might lie ahead. And as they went into the glen proper, Somerled looked at Anna, and he saw that her face was silver with tears. Yet it was not sadness either; he knew it was not sadness that made those tears.

She had grown there; she had been born and had grown in that place, and she saw in front of her as she walked those who had watched over her when she was sick, those who had taught and corrected her, those who had wept for her when she was lost. And all of them walked now in silence and in this act of love, all the way to the bottom of the path that led to the house Somerled had made.

Then, without words, those who held branches gathered and created an arch under which the two passed. They bowed their heads and passed, but they had to stop and turn before they were gone inside, to thank with their eyes for all that this meant.

And he stood above Anna on the path and held his arms around her, and her hands rose to hold his. And slowly the procession began back to the village, and he felt the tears warm on her face.

They went inside at last, half-dead with tiredness. And

everywhere they looked there were gifts, some opened and some still wrapped, but none of it mattered now. It felt strange being there at last; they were like children and almost shy, for suddenly the journey was over, and there was nothing more that needed to be done.

Gently he brought her round to face him, and held her hands together in his own, and smoothed the gold softness at her brow.

'There needs to be nothing tonight,' he breathed. 'We have all our lives.'

And she searched his face, to know he was sure, and nodded, relieved. For there had been no real rest for long days, and at home there had been searches and questions and quarrels.

They went to the bedroom and did not even close the curtains. They undressed each other, silent and slow, learning things they did not know, until both stood white in the beginning of the new day. And all that they had between them, all that remained, was the thin circlet of gold that was her wedding ring. And he touched it with one finger.

'That was the gift I had to make,' he told her. 'Gold from under the falls at the top of the glen. I found it myself.'

And she turned it and the tiny light of the new day was caught in its gold. And she kissed him then, deep and true, as they lay together that first time. And they slept and did not sleep; held one another and touched, lay still a time and then remembered, fell together once more. And it was enough; it was a kind of sea crossing, a voyage into a strange land, so they seemed not to waken in the same place at all. And late in the morning she touched his left arm and he opened his eyes at once, wide-awake and wondering.

'Look, Somerled,' she breathed.

And he raised his head, and three deer that had been grazing close to the window were startled and scattered away on flint hooves. And he wanted to sleep once more but now he was awake.

They got to know each other that day. They knew all the big things from before, but there were the little things to learn. How this or that was preferred, and sometimes the story that lay behind. And a lot of the day was laughter, nothing but the celebration of silliness and the joy in each other's presence. She opened presents, from lost aunts and half-forgotten friends, and then there was the gift from her parents, and that they had to open together.

May your love stay warm all the days that are yours.

And they found that it was all they might ever need for their fireside, half a dozen fine-wrought tools melted and hammered by Allan. But at the bottom of it all was something else, and Anna gasped. It was a roll of notes, bound up with pieces of white string.

'It's from Aunt Jessie. You know, the old soul that's stayed with us since I was twelve. She has no one of her own and this is her way of saying thank you. It'll help us, Somerled, it'll help us over the winter.'

He thought of that as he went to fish later that afternoon. Strange to be going to fish, he knew, but it had been the perfect day – a smur of rain on the wind, and just the best breeze. A few flying things still in the air, and he guessed that high loch of his would fish late.

But it was Anna who had persuaded him; she said she wanted to make the kitchen hers, to unwrap the last of the presents. And if he came back with a fish, so much the better, for they had little else in the house.

So he went, and thought as he walked of her words about winter. She had said she would serve still in the inn, but he knew that his heart struggled with that. He wanted her to himself, that was true, but perhaps there lay something else inside. The fear that he couldn't feed them himself, that struggled somewhere deep within. Even Aunt Jessie's goodness was not what he wanted to trust in.

And as he walked, out of the trees and into the great field of rocks, he thought of the childhood he had known. A big house and land, the place where the Stewarts had lived five generations and more. But at school he had sat by the window, yearning to be out in the hills and the lochs and the wild of it all. It had breathed in him; he felt the blood of the land and he heard it, under his feet. And in the end they gave up beating fractions and exports and currencies into his head, and they let him play with wood and stone and metal as much as they could. And when he got home he was out, out into miles of sea woods and horses and moorland. There had only once been talk of university, and never again.

He came to the heights above the last of the rocks and looked all around. The autumn was burning away; the last light lay here and there, but it was dark and dying. The high hills were like crystals, grey-blue jags of rock. The wind whispered around him and he waited until his breath was back. Now it was the sea of the heather, but at least he had the loch in his sights.

He came at last to the little beach, and his first thought was of wood. What new pieces of strangeness might the bog have given up? Mostly they were small bits, fit only for lighting the fire – but there was an owl asleep in that white-blue fragment, and maybe there was an otter in the longer, darker one. He put them safe where he would remember them and made ready the rod.

It was so long since he had cast he was afraid he would catch nothing more than a cold. He stood in the wrong place to begin with and tangled the flies and was vexed at himself. He went to a rock on the far shore and that was better, but always he had his eyes on the island. That was what called to him, and he wondered if he could . . .

He well knew that some lochs were shallow at the edge and then, all at once, went down to the depths. He knew too that there were lochs whose peaty floors would suck down a horse. He went like a blind man, cautious and watching, ready to reach back at the first scent of danger. He went out four feet, and six, and he was all but halfway to the island. For the loch was long and thin, shaped like a fin, and the island was the same at its heart.

The water was all but up to his waist now, but he didn't feel the cold and the breeze would dry him in time. He decided it was safe to go on, and three steps later he was rising, splashing out onto the jumble of stones there at the islet's end. And before he had looked up, his eyes caught something there among the rocks. It was the shape that drew him, for the other stones were all of the same size, round and smooth like polished fists. But this stone was long, and the mottled back of it was shaped and had a sharp edge. He set down the rod and bent for it with trembling hands, and it was just what he had thought it – an axe. The one tool he had carried out of the west, but made of metal and from a new world that could pour out any number of others. This had been one alone, made perhaps by the man who had come here to cut wood. And Somerled looked all around him at the ring of hills, and he saw not a single habitation, and he thought that after all these thousands of years so much had changed and yet so little.

He caught one fish, a strong trout that fought at the end of the line until at last he brought it up out of its element and broke it on the stones. Beautiful it looked with its sheen of colours in the low grey light. He was glad he had brought the canvas bag to carry it, for the fish fell from his grasp several times before he got back to the end of the loch, so slippery was its skin.

The rain came in earnest before he was back, and he all but lost his balance badly when clattering among the rocks. The house was buried in mist and he had to guess his way towards it through the trees. And he looked forward to seeing her; it had been good up there in that place he loved, but what price returning home? And she came to him, smiling, wiping her hands on a cloth.

'I've missed you,' she murmured, pushing him in to their room.

'I've a fish,' he said, holding out the bag. 'And I need to find dry things.'

'But I have to reward the fisherman,' she said. And she made him lie on his back, and she took away all his clothes with their twigs and heather. And then he was naked at last and she swept off her own clothes and lay over him, and he closed his eyes at the wonder of it, and kissed her wherever he reached, and their faces met and held together. And she brought shocks from him and long thrills of pleasure, and at last he caught her and brought her down beside him and his hands were buried in the soft gold of her hair.

And they rode the waves of this, over and over, until there was no more in them and they were washed up on a new shore, shy and content and tired. And she said she was starving, and they laughed.

He gutted the trout and got it ready, and there was wine that had been given for the wedding that was still not drunk. And they sat together and had a feast, talking about everything and nothing.

'They're fine, they're very fine,' said Allan. 'They're so fine I'm afraid that no one's going to buy them!'

And he laughed and shook his head, that great bear of a man, but he laughed alone. Somerled couldn't laugh.

When Allan held the otter and the wren in his two hands they looked the size of acorns. The two men stood together in the blacksmith's yard where two young boys, apprentices, thumped away at lumps of metal. Even on this day in early November it was too hot in there.

'Come and sit with me a moment,' Allan said, his face suddenly serious again. He set the two figures down on a tiny table and drew up a chair for his son-in-law. He himself just leaned over, kind and generous.

'You've a fine hand for carving, Somerled. Let no one tell you otherwise. But think on it, who's going to buy such finery in the glen? Maybe if we lived close to London they could find a place at the markets, and Arabs and all manner of others might buy them. But these are working folk in the glen, and most of them have never thought of such finery . . .'

'Yes – finery, finery, finery – it's the third time you've said it!'

Somerled rose in fury and swept the otter and the wren to the floor.

'I'm asking you then what I should do instead! I have to make sufficient for Anna and me, and I have to do it with these two hands.'

He sat once more; crouched, almost, in the chair. And Allan's giant hand returned to his shoulder and his voice was soft. With the other hand he gently picked up the carvings from the floor.

'You make the things they need. The things they send to town for, and toys, toys for the children. Make many things. And I've a side room here at the smiddy can be yours for a shop. You don't need to stand there yourself; you can bring down what you make and I'll keep an eye on the place for you. You can give me the odd fish as a thank you. Anna said the last one was a fair treat.'

Somerled swallowed and got up, ashamed and embarrassed, and shook the hand of the blacksmith. He had no more words. That had been sufficient. He saw the truth of what Allan said, but it maddened him all the same. It was these things he wanted to find. He wanted to make beautiful creations.

But he bought cheap wood and he made cheap things. Wooden spoons for children teething, and napkin rings, and little giants for boys to play with. He made them fast and he made them crudely, and all of them sold in the village before the week had passed.

Anna gathered the coins in front of her and touched his sleeve with her hand. She looked at him and he would not look at her.

'You should be proud, not ashamed! This is enough for all I need in the next days! What would you do otherwise? Travel at five in the morning to work in the mill in town? You go every morning up the finest hill in the glen that's different every day, and you do what you want to do!'

'No, that's not what I want to do! I want to make beautiful things, and I'm reduced to making rubbish! Can't you see that?'

What she could see were the tears that stood in his eyes. She got up and smoothed his back, the hunched anger of his shoulders. She whispered to him and brought him back from his darkness. She reached out for his hand and he opened his own to take it.

'Don't give up. Maybe my father's wrong, or perhaps things will change. If you become known for your carving, and even beyond the glen, who knows what might be possible. Give it time, Somerled, give it time!'

He gave it time and tried to shut out his impatience. To heal his own fever he walked to one of the bigger lochs to gather bogwood. Up at the top of the shore were more knots of ebony- and dark tan- and bronze-coloured wood than ever he could have carried back with him. With trembling hands he searched them, searched for the creatures that might sleep there. He saw things almost at once; he had only to turn the branch a single time to know. It was a fine enough haul he

41

returned with, but it frustrated him that he couldn't set to work. The best piece of all held an eagle, the wide span of it, and his hands ached to find it. But what was the point? It would take a night and a day, and in that time he could have carved half a week's worth of dross. He opened the bag he had brought home in the House of the Sparrow, and he turned the pieces with longing. It was dark and he sat there in the darkness, as the wind blew cold about them and the sleet fell.

Anna was asleep when he came in, and he folded in softly to the bed so as not to waken her, and turned away. His eyes blinked against the silence and the night, and he hugged in to the turmoil of his thoughts. It was long before sleep swept him away.

But when he did sleep he travelled through strange dreams. He was with his father and he was cutting down a tree. His father was using the axe he had inherited from his father, the axe that Somerled had brought to the glen. But as the blows landed one after one, blood began to run from the cut in the trunk; not resin, blood. Yet Somerled's father went on and on cutting relentlessly; the blows becoming faster and faster, until Somerled began screaming.

'What is it?'

He woke to the utter stillness of the room and Anna's hand on his chest. He breathed deep a long time as he lay there.

'Nothing.'

Yet in the morning the strange thing was that there was something. He remembered Deirdre and wondered again where it could be that she had written from and where she could have gone back to. What if he were to write to her and send it to the old house? He didn't even know if his parents lived there any longer, but the post office would recognise the name. They might have a forwarding address, even if he didn't. It was worth a try.

He had carved a whole box-load of new things by lunch-time and was in need of more wood. He got out paper and pen and sat there – how long was it since he had written a letter to his own sister? And as he thought of that it came back to him from a dark recess of memory; he saw himself sitting in a corner of his own room in the old house, writing a repentant letter to his sister. For she had again been favoured by their father and he had felt shut out and small, and he had put a worm down her back. He knew she hated worms more than anything in the world, and he had had to search long and hard to find a big one.

Now he was writing to say he was sorry, but he was more sorry for the poor hand that had been smacked and smacked by his mother. It throbbed as he sat there holding the pen . . .

'Somerled, are you needing anything from the village?'

He looked up, startled, as though he had been found out. He stared and then smiled; shook his head and then remembered.

'Those are all ready for the shop! And you could bring me new wood if you can carry it. I'm writing to Deirdre, to my sister.'

She had glanced at the page. He looked at her and thought of the first time he saw her. He wondered if she had changed. He was too close to see. She was thinking about something and he didn't know what it was. He was going to ask and then he didn't.

She was gone and after the struggle of the first line it

flowed. He even reminded her of that letter all those years ago, and he smiled as he wrote the words. He found himself writing that he wanted to go back with her, back to the house. He was about to ask her if she had news of their parents, but somehow that was too much. Too much for both of them. But he said he hoped they could go back, together – that he wouldn't go on his own. And then he thought of the one side of her face, distorted and melted away. She had said she would tell him, but not then, not there. And he thought again of his dream of the tree.

He finished and put the letter in an envelope. It was strange writing his old address; there was part of him that had thought he would never write it again. And then he held the envelope and wondered if he might never hear a word more. He could do nothing but see what happened.

A fine hail was falling and he went and stood outside. A whole net of it misted the lower glen and the hills did not vanish, they grew thin and ghostly. He wondered if Anna had wanted him to go with her, if it was that that had been wrong. But then why hadn't she said something?

The winter was coming and there was so much to do. And he thought of his carving, the real carving he wanted to be done, and he knew there would be no time. And a sadness he could not share crept like a bear into its cave inside him.

It was to be a long winter. That was what the famers said; it was what the gamekeepers and the factors said. The first snow came in November, and it pattered sideways against the drystone walls and it drove against the windows. And now the hills vanished; they were swallowed in a wool-white nothing that drove eastwards and did not stop for two long days. He stood at the side window and watched it. He had always watched snow, perhaps because they had had so little of it in the west. Their bit of land jutted out into the sea, water on both sides of it and a beach at its end. There was snow plenty deeper in where the land rose into wild hills, but not there on that promontory of land that was low and salty – nothing ever lay there. Not enough at least to keep him out of school.

Now he watched the snow and was a child again. There was something of him that wanted to be snowed in, even though he was grown now and had to think of firewood and light and food. The child rose again in him and peeped up on tiptoe to see the driving white against the windows.

That night the stove was filled. Its window gleamed like the single eye of some mythical beast. They sat in the room he had made of wood and stone, and outside the darkness raged. He was reading an old book, something he remembered from childhood, except that it had changed. There was a part of him that wished he had left it as it had been. He had reached that point and knew he would not read any further, but still he held the book open in his hands and still his eyes bent to the page. Yet he knew that Anna was watching him, that her eyes were fixed on him. He looked up.

'I want to have a child,' she murmured. And there was everything in her voice: longing, love, loss, loneliness, and more he did not know. He nodded and they both got up. They did all that had to be done and left the stove to its roaring. They crept into a freezing bed and held one another and she cried. He held her as she cried and asked her nothing. They said no more that night though they lay there awake a long

45

time. And sometimes it was as though her crying was part of the storm, and the two wove into one.

The following morning she was white and trembling and far away. He was kind and generous; there was nothing more to be carved and he could think of his own things – he might even have time to get back to the carving he loved. He brought her breakfast and made soft the pillows behind her head and kneeled down beside her.

'That was it, you know,' she said, and looked at somewhere beyond him.

He tried to guess what she meant and couldn't.

She looked at him, eyes strong and sure. 'A child.'

And he nodded, foolish – happy and afraid.

He had to go into the village later that day and the track had all but vanished. It had stopped snowing; the sky was an eerie patterning of white and grey. There wasn't a sound in the whole world except the noise of his boots. The village was a Christmas card; the roads hadn't been cleared and the school was closed. He met with a gale of children shrieking down to the post office, and a snowball missed his ear. He went in to see if there were any letters.

'Just the one, but it's been delivered by hand. I'm trying to think who it was who brought it. Can you remember, George?'

He already recognised his sister's writing. That was faster than he had believed possible, and in all this winter too. He was so impatient to know what she had said that he went into the church to read it. He stamped the snow from his boots. Inside, there was a heavy scent he couldn't work out, thick and dusty. He sat in one of the front pews, in at the side.

The tearing of the envelope echoed, somehow seemed much louder there in that place.

Somerled,
I am writing this quickly and can say no more than that. Your letter came this morning; it was sent by our old postman, John Ferguson – he was the only one I trusted with my address.

I'd like to go back with you, this winter, if possible. I may not be able to again. There would be time at the end of this month, but I know it might be difficult for you because of the weather. A friend is going west on the 24th and I could travel with him.

Send me your answer right away; tell the post office the letter must be given to Neil. They'll do the rest.

With love and blessings, and all my good wishes to Anna,
Deirdre O'Neill

He scanned the lines again and again. Then, in the silence of the church, he heard a dry flickering sound. He looked up and searched; a frayed tortoiseshell butterfly was there against the stained-glass window. He would have got up and caught it and let it out, but what was the point? At least here there was light and warmth.

He looked again at the letter. O'Neill. There was so much he didn't know. And all at once he was aware of being watched. He glanced up and saw the minister, and got up, the paper crumpling in his hands.

He explained himself like an awkward boy; realised afterwards there had been no reason to say anything at all. But the minister smiled and waved it away, came and sat down with him a moment.

'And how's Anna?'

He said at once that she was fine; the words were out before he had thought of them. And then he remembered how he had left her, how she had been in the last days. But he could say nothing of that.

'You know that her growing up was hard?'

He looked up surprised. That house with its laughter and kindness, with all its talk and generosity. How could it have been?

'I was a young man when Anna was growing up, when she was still in primary school. Allan and Martha used to have me in on Sundays, after the service. I felt welcome and I enjoyed the noise at the table; I used to think there was nowhere else I laughed like that. But I saw that often Anna sat outside it all. There seemed a sadness about her that was missed. Oh, make no mistake, she was loved. But there was something there that went untouched and forgotten. Maybe it was easier for me to see because I came from somewhere else. But that's why I ask, and I'll come and see you in the glen, though not before all this has gone! And they say it'll be a while yet!'

And they got up together, Somerled folding the letter into his pocket. And he heard again the flickering of the butterfly. And he thanked the minister, even though he wasn't sure why he did, and went out into the new brightness of the day. The white skies had torn and there was a stretch of blue there.

He knew that he would have to send an answer to Deirdre right away, and that meant having to make the decision alone.

Surely Anna would understand? Deirdre had said this chance might never come again, and he suddenly thought that this might be the last time he'd see her. There were so many questions to so many questions.

They wouldn't let him buy a single postcard and an envelope; they insisted he use up old stock. He simply scribbled a note saying he'd make his own way to the west to meet her, and he put her name on the envelope – that strange surname that told him nothing either.

'George, this is going back to the fellow, whoever he is, who knows where my sister lives. Will you get it to him just as soon as possible? I'm happy to pay for it. Many, many thanks to you both!'

He knew he should call in on Allan and Martha, but he wanted to tell Anna what he had decided right away. He chased back through the snow, and when he came to the point where he turned to go right up the hill, he saw that another set of footprints went on. Who on earth? He looked ahead and the prints continued into the distance, until he could follow them no longer. For some reason it unnerved him. It might have been a walker; it might have been a farmer out to check on livestock; it might have been anyone – yet those small prints in the snow made him feel strange.

And then Anna was there beside him and she hugged him.

'Did you bring me milk or potatoes or flour or bread? No, not a thing, but you brought yourself home and I'm glad of that.'

He said nothing, but pointed at the steps running up into the glen. She shook her head and put her hands on her hips.

'I saw no one passing. But it was a real person, Somerled.

Ghosts don't wear shoes. Come in and have a cup of tea with me.'

And he followed her and noticed the way that even now she walked differently, more carefully, and not simply because of the snow. And he looked up and saw her in front of him before the house, and his eyrie of solitude beyond, and a thrill passed through him, and he remembered. Inside he brought out the letter and unfolded it, and told her how amazed he was there had been an answer at all, and how it would be just a few days over there, but what a chance it would be! And she was happy for him, he could see that; she said that of course he must go and that she would be all right.

Then he went up to the House of the Sparrow and carved all he could while the light lasted. He carved longer than that, until his eyes hurt with the strain. But he had another box-load to take into the village the next day, and he went down the steps into the house and found her just as he had left her earlier, the cup still held in her left hand. He told her the box was done, that he'd go down first thing in the morning with it, and bring back what he'd forgotten today. And she nodded and he asked what it was and she shook her head. She got up and went away into the kitchen to make their supper.

He wondered just how he would get west. He reckoned it would take him two days, and for that reason he would have to start earlier than Deirdre. He was glad most of all because he had found her again. There had been such enmity between them; no, perhaps resentment more than enmity. He barely remembered saying goodbye to her when he left. He had not cared then if he never saw any of them again.

He wondered where they would stay. The village – a post

office, a hotel and a scattering of houses by the old jetty – was half a mile south of where they had grown up. He thought suddenly of the money, the money it would take to go west and to stay there for those days. They had so little to spare. But this might never happen again; it was a chance that had to be taken or lost.

After supper she sat and looked into the window of the stove. Then her eyes danced and she caught his hand and put it on her stomach. 'D'you think it's a boy or a girl? And we haven't even thought of names yet!'

He shook his head. None of it had truly sunk in. 'Have you told your parents yet? I can imagine your mother . . .'

She smiled. 'That's why I haven't told them. Not until the danger's over. She'll fuss over me like a mother hen and there'll be time enough for that. And whatever I say the whole village'll know once they know.'

He smiled and nodded. Martha with a secret would be like a child with sweets. It would hardly be destined to stay her own for long.

She suddenly turned to look at him. 'Will you tell your parents if you find them when you go west?'

He thought about it. He didn't even know if they were alive. 'I left in such anger,' he said. And as he spoke the words flickers of that day went through his head and he wanted to sweep them away.

'I'll decide when I'm there,' he said. 'At the moment I'm just glad I've met Deirdre and that we can go back together. I'd never have gone alone. When I was growing up I somehow felt I was the only one, that it was just my struggle. The more I think of it, the more I realise she struggled too.'

Anna nodded. 'And we all carry those things later, all our lives.'

The following day he went down early to the village. Allan had time only to take the box before getting back to his hammering; there was a job to be finished by that afternoon. But Somerled dared to go in to see Martha and she clucked about him, filling him with baking and asking about this and asking about that. And Aunt Jessie was there; she sat wheezing in the window, half-reading a book and half-looking up to smile. And as he watched her when Martha was fussing over the kettle it came to him that he'd never really talked to her and had no idea now where to begin. But he remembered her gift to them and wondered how long she'd saved to find all those notes.

'Now that's half a dozen eggs, Somerled, but they're older and you must remember to tell Anna they're for baking. And I have an extra loaf and just a few scones for you. Oh, and I nearly forgot – there's money here for you! That's for what was sold last week, and Allan won't take a penny of it so don't even think about it. I'll fight you, Somerled, I'll fight and I'll win!'

So he left with a whole pocketful of money. He bought Anna a little bag of toffees before he left, for it was a treat she'd never have afforded herself. As he went he imagined what it would be like going back west in a week's time and the thought thrilled his heart. Here he had everything but the sea. He had grown up with his own beach; however bad it was at home, there had always been the sea. Never the same and never predictable; every time bringing new treasure. It had been his best friend, he saw now, and it had never crossed his mind before.

Two days later he woke up very early in the morning and couldn't get back to sleep. He slid away from Anna and dressed, padded about the house in the greyness. It had frozen hard overnight; it would be a clear and perfect day. He nearly went out to begin carving early and then hadn't the heart; sometimes the old bitterness at what he had to produce was too much. He had to be glad it made money for them, but that was all.

He thought of the loch and suddenly wanted to be there. It would be a battle to get there; heaven only knew how long it might take. He scribbled a note to Anna and left it for her in the kitchen; then he put on his boots and was gone.

When he was up in the wood and saw the old pines laden with their carvings of snow and ice, he thought of wolves. This had been a place of wolves. And the thought of the man out on the island, the one whose axe he had found, and he thought how he would have heard the wolves below him in the woods.

He scrabbled and slid over the great boulders above the wood. When he reached the plateau he did as he always did and stopped, looked around him in every direction. There was not a sound under the white-blue of the skies. He looked down at his own glen and his eye ran up to the falls where he had found the gold for Anna's ring. But his eye did not rest there, it went on over the great ramparts of the hills into another narrow glen he had never seen before, and the white eye of a frozen loch. He had noticed none of it before, and all at once he remembered the footprints he had not known, and even there in the perfect stillness of that white-blue day he felt again the passing of that shadow.

Had he truly known just how hard it would be to reach his loch he might never have started out. He lost count of the number of times he fell, once onto the side of a rock with the edge of his hip bone. But he had started out and he was determined to get there.

A little cluster of ptarmigan flew away into the white air as he floundered the last of the yards. And now he saw that his loch was frozen; it lay glazed and strange in the early day. He went down to the shore and, without thinking, looked to see if there were any new pieces of bogwood. Nothing. He went forward and put one foot cautiously onto the ice, waiting for it to splinter. To his surprise he found it hard as a glass pavement. He had not guessed it would have been so cold here; he didn't think of it as that much higher than the house. He knew at once he could stand there on the ice; he did so, afraid still there might come snaps and cracks from all round the edge. Nothing. It was so solid he was able to walk along the middle of the loch, all the way to the island.

He thought of the child that Anna and he were to have. Part of him rejoiced and part of him was afraid. He remembered his own childhood and did not want to remember. He wondered suddenly if he would be a good father and he felt a flicker of fear through him.

Perhaps he would find answers, find something of his own lost self, when he went west with Deirdre. He hoped so. He prayed so. He looked down at his feet, saw the place where he had found the stone axe.

Anna came with him to the village, had packed a box for him: new-baked rolls, an egg, some of the last plums from her parents' tree, and a piece of toffee from the packet he himself had bought her. And there was a flask of good, sweet tea. They were standing at the chestnut tree, at the crossroads. All the children were there too, in a miserable huddle that Monday morning, for they stayed at the boarding house through the week. He was telling her that he would telephone if he found a call-box, and she was telling him that she might stay down with her parents for a night of two, rather than be alone in the empty house. And they talked over each other as the bus came, and its wheels dipped into the churned-up snow. Not a second late it was, and he kissed her and she called something he never heard, and then he was swept up in the struggle of the children to get on board in time. He looked backwards and saw for a flicker the white oval of her face, before the bus turned and began thundering east along the slush of the straight road. He was both excited and frightened, felt suddenly younger than he was.

He opened his bag, not for food but to look at the two carvings he had brought with him: the otter and the wren. He wanted to give Deirdre the otter, for he remembered their searches for otters in a cave down close to the beach. There had been a brief window of time when they were friends as children; something had happened with their father that drew them together. Their mother was relentlessly hard on them both; Somerled could do no right in her eyes. What hurt most was her iciness. The dismissive steel-blue of her eyes. The way things were waved away. The power of a single look. Their father simply favoured Deirdre, except that favour was too poor a word. He wanted the best for her, doted on her, fought for her, was constantly anxious for her. Somerled sometimes felt he was all but invisible to him; his father would pass him and brush him aside, or else meet the two of them and bend down at once to Deirdre, all kindness and concern.

He touched the carving of the otter and knew he should give it to Deirdre. But it was the best he had ever made, and the wren was less precious. Yet in thinking that through in his head, he knew the otter had to be hers.

He sat on the bus the whole way to Pitnacraig and the railway station. He got out, hearing the thud of his own heart, for how many years was it since he had been on a train? A weak sun melted the thick grey roof of cloud and he stood there, in a pool of cold light. He had a whole hour to wait for the train. There was no one else on the platform, though he could see the shadows moving about in the station office, and hear the mumble of voices. He bought his ticket and went and swept the snow from a seat on the northbound side of the track. He had a precious cup of tea from the flask, and as he opened the lid and the scent rose to him, he was back in the kitchen in the glen. And it was not only the scent, it was the melding of a hundred things: sounds and tastes and the scents of other things also. It was not that he wanted to be back there, but at that moment it was like a beautiful cave, and it was good simply to know that it was there, that he would return.

The hour was up at last, and by then another five souls had come to wait. Two of them were children with their mother, and they asked endless questions about the journey. No sooner had one answer been given but the next question came. Once he looked up and met the mother's eyes and they smiled at each other.

He found a window-seat and didn't read the books that he

had brought. He wanted the journey: the rivers, the woods, the hills. When someone asked him about a newspaper, he was so far away the person had to repeat the question. But sometimes he went beyond the landscape, acted out the return to the house with his sister. As he went up the drive in his mind, he was a child once more. All that had haunted him flooded back. And his parents came out; they were as he had seen them last but they had not changed. And he did not know what to say to them.

In Strathspey the snow was half a foot deeper. The train dragged through, snaking past frozen lochs and pine forest encrusted with snow. And the Cairngorms came into view, and at first he thought they were white clouds. They became as he looked at them the long, grey forms of wolves, stretching into a far kingdom.

In Inverness he had almost two hours to wait. The station was cold and unappealing, so he walked out into the town. He wanted to see the castle and the River Ness; it was a chance he wouldn't have for long enough again.

When he passed the post office, right there at the heart of the town, he looked in at a shop selling the finest clothes. He was about to look away when his eye caught at one side a display-stand of sculptures. There were many tiers to the stand; on one level were leaping salmon, so real one felt the quivering of their driven bodies. On another level sat a pert red squirrel, holding a hazelnut in its paws. But as he looked at the squirrel, Somerled saw that it was not a sculpture at all. It was a carving wrought from red-tinged wood.

He took out his own carvings of the wren and the otter and held them in his right hand so they knocked together. Should he? He had never done something like this before in his life, yet it was the chance he had mourned not having. He went back and opened the door.

'Yes, sir.'

He was not sure if the words of the English voice were a question or an accusation. He was aware of his scuffed shoes, the pack on his back. He babbled something about where he had come from and where he was going. At the end of it all the tall, gloved gentleman said that he wasn't the right person to speak to but that he would call the manager. And he gave Somerled a thin, oily smile.

.   In the end the manager came out. He was slow and fat and wore wire-rimmed spectacles, and he said nothing and did not smile at all. Somerled babbled again, but this time about what he did for a living and how sometimes he had time for proper carvings like these. He put the wren and the otter onto the glass-topped surface of the desk and the man picked them up and turned them and looked at them without his glasses. Somerled said some more about the beauty of the place where they lived and the richness of the natural world around them.

'How much would you want for these?'

He had never thought of that before and blurted a figure without giving himself time to think.

'That's far too much. Half it and you have a reasonable price. We take fifty per cent in commission. And if you live any distance from Inverness you'll have to post things to us, and include the postage for what might have to be returned.'

Somerled asked, in broken phrases, how many carvings he might expect to sell in a year.

'Well, I'm no fortune teller. But we sell to many of the estate owners in the Highlands. And if they like things they come back to us. They want gifts for friends in London; they want to take back anything that represents the Highlands. But if it sells, we'll come back to you for more. It's as simple as that. Make sense?'

Somerled nodded. The manager said nothing more, but muttered something to the tall assistant and then vanished once more into the back premises. The oily smile returned.

'Anything else I can help you with, sir?'

He was about to say no when he had the presence of mind to remember something. He had neither the name nor the address of the premises.

The tall man went to the other end of the desk and picked up a sheet of paper, leaned forward and handed it to Somerled.

In his nervous state Somerled almost forgot to retrieve the otter and the wren. He closed the great glass door behind him and stepped back onto the pavement. His heart sang within him. He wanted to tell Anna right away, there and then! His hands shook with nerves and elation.

All the way to Kyle of Lochalsh he drifted in and out of sleep. He had carved things and they had sold; he was telling Anna and she was rejoicing – he could live from carving fine things! And the House of the Sparrow was full of the creatures he had found; and he had become faster at carving, he could finish three in a day . . .

The land he passed through was wild with winter. He saw not one living soul the whole of the way, only ruin after ruin and a herd of red deer battling their way along the edge of

a river that was bearded with ice. They had fled from the
clatter of the train, and they stood now and watched as it
curved away. And he thought of those who had come like
him with little more than an axe to build a life among the
hills. And he thought of the winters, and the hunger, and
the children. He looked out at the books of their lives, written in Gaelic, and it was as though the train passed slow
through that snowscape in homage to them. For they were
gone, and they had not succeeded. They had been defeated
in the end, and every story was different. And he thought of
the story he wrote himself, and of the child who was coming
too and who would be part of it, and he wondered what the
ending would be. For every one who came with an axe ready
to begin believed they were blessed, that their story would
end happily. And it was not so.

Then they came through the last of the hills and there was
the sea. His heart thrilled in him and he sat on the other side
of the train to press his face to the window. He caught little
glimpses, of coves half-hidden by rowans, and full scythes of
rocky beaches. And the beaches were white, not with foam but
snow. He never remembered the beach at home with snow.
And he saw a boat and thought of how he had gone out with
Roddy Norman for lobsters. They had caught nothing but it
had been the joy of it and the stories he had heard. Then, all
of a sudden, they were into Kyle and there was the smell of
the water and the shrieking of gulls; boxes being off-loaded;
and Gaelic being thrown about as easy as laughter. And there
was Deirdre.

'Somerled, this is Murdo, a good friend from Inverness,
and he has kindly said he will drive us down the coast. He's

quite right, it would have taken us for ever to get to the house otherwise.'

Somerled shook the hand that was bigger than his own.

'But how did you know I'd be on this train?'

'I think there are two from Inverness,' said Deirdre and smiled. 'I had a good idea.'

He sat in the back and it must have taken them an hour. All the windows were steamed up in the tiny car, and Murdo kept dabbing at the windscreen in front of him and trying to peer through. He was much too big for the car; he sat there like a bullock, restless and saying things that might have been words, and Deirdre talked to him and turned round to Somerled.

When they got out of the car with their luggage he recognised nothing for a moment because of the snow. She went and stood beside him.

'There's the promontory; the house is hidden behind the trees. And down there, just below us, is where you once wanted to have a rope. There was a rowan tree and you wanted a rope swing and our mother said no. I think there was a boat there at one time too ...'

'Yes, I remember! Because there were sea urchins under it. You could put your hand underneath the wood on the outer edge and you could find sea urchins! I know where we are; of course I do!'

And out there was the islet he had never reached. It was about a mile into the bay and there was a cove of white sand held between two promontories facing the mainland. When he was really miserable, when he was at the end of himself, he would shout through his tears that he was going to live on Shuna.

It was the only time his mother ever smiled; just and no more.

'Well, I hope you have plenty to eat there,' she'd say.

And he had no answer and he would fall up the stairs to his room and look out through the blur of them at the island. He would make a boat and he would go and live there and be at peace . . .

'Come on,' Deirdre said. 'I asked Murdo to drop us here first. Then I thought we could walk up to the hotel.'

'The hotel?' he echoed.

'Yes, my treat. I have money that I feel guilty about, so at least now and again I can be generous.'

They turned and the old hotel was behind them, on the other side of the drive and up a long, winding track. There had been a chestnut tree, he remembered. It was the only one and all the boys came from school. Charlie, the gardener, was for ever chasing them away.

But he wondered what to say to Deirdre; watched her just ahead of him on the path. He saw the one side of her face, the side that was intact. There were so many things he didn't know; so many blocked paths. He searched among a rubble of questions for what he might ask.

'How long is it since you left?'

They crossed the road and started up the track to the hotel. Still she said nothing and he almost wondered if she had heard him; but she was thinking, trying to work it out.

'I suppose it was a year after you. A year or eighteen months.'

Suddenly she stopped and turned to him. And it was the first time he had seen her face in daylight. The one half was unchanged; just as he remembered it. All the pictures he had told half the truth.

'And I don't want to talk about anything now, about anything in the life I have. We're here for this, nothing more. So please don't ask.'

He nodded and she went ahead of him. He saw vaguely that the snow had almost no tracks. He thought of the strangeness of it all.

He had never stayed in a hotel in his life. Once they had been here, for his father's birthday, and he and Deirdre had been allowed lemonade. It had been a hot day in July; the air woollen and heavy.

Now a log fire burned in the grate. The lobby smelled of pipe smoke; the tartan carpets were frayed. He wondered how they were able to keep the place open at all when it was so quiet, and at that very moment he heard the woman behind the desk explaining they had a large shooting party over from Germany. They were out for the day in the hills. The woman led the way upstairs and before Somerled went into his room Deirdre asked if they might meet in half an hour. He nodded. At once he went to the window and creaked it open. He looked down and out over his own childhood. There was so much there. It was like opening a cupboard he had locked years before so all manner of things tumbled from it.

'The house is let out in the summer months by the estate,' Deirdre told him, when she came to find him, and he understood she must be talking about their house, their home. 'It's all shut up at the moment, but we'll try and find a way in.'

Yet he wasn't sure if he wanted to, if he had the courage. It was like opening an old wound wide, so it would hurt once more. But he couldn't tell her. They walked fast, down the track and onto the road and along it. All the way to the old metal sign and the start of the track down to the house. To Davaar.

The rhododendrons, the oak, the steep part of the drive where he used to make a slide. It was like walking through a dream, and the ghosts of stories came at him from every side. But most of them were his own; they had been his world and his salvation. Inside were the locked bars of the dark things, all that he had run away from when he went east, walking and walking until he reached the glen.

They came to the back wall of the house and already Deirdre was searching. The handle of the door screeched, but it was locked tight. She looked up and around, searching for an answer he almost prayed she might not find. And what had happened to their parents? She had told him nothing about them though it was obvious they were not there. Then she looked round at him, suddenly smiling.

'D'you remember the bathroom at the back? The little one? We used to creep out of that window because it opened so quietly!'

She went over to the left and tried it. The window slid open, smooth and still. Already she was climbing in over the sill. He'd have to follow. He stood there beside her, his hands shaking. All at once she took them in her own, lifted them and made him look at her.

'They're not here, Somerled. They're gone; it's over. We need to do this to free ourselves, to find answers.'

He would have said something, but she had gone ahead of him, out into the corridor. He knew she would go to the

64

sea room, and as he walked he thought his chest might burst. A weak winter sun filled the room, and the air danced with dust. The dust of their lives, he thought. The dust of all the shouting and the anger and the pain. What had it been for? What had the years of it been for?

Far away in his mind he heard a piano. He looked over to the left-hand corner of the room and saw himself practising scales on a piano that was no longer there. His feet didn't touch the floor and he was wearing shorts. And his mother was walking across the floor behind, tapping a ruler against the fingers of her right hand – the ruler she used to bring down on his hands when he did not get things right.

All at once he realised that Deirdre had been talking, that she was still talking. She was standing over at the window, looking out.

'. . . and I used to envy the fact that you got away from the house so much. You were out there and you were better at all these things than I was. I never knew how to catch a sea urchin or to gut one; I couldn't catch fish. So I yearned to be out there, but once I was, I almost felt trapped, helpless. And because we were so often at daggers drawn, it meant I had to be here on my own.'

She turned to look at him now and he nodded, under-standing.

'You're right. We could have been allies and joined forces, but we never did. Somehow it just didn't seem an option; maybe that's even the way they wanted it to be.'

She came back and stood beside him, looked at the same dust that circled in the air.

'I don't even think she wanted children, you know. It was

all about conformity. And they had two children, a boy and a girl. They had done what was ordained. Perhaps he did – at least he wanted a girl.'

She went out of the room as if she could bear it no longer. Her last words still echoed in his head as he followed her.

'What d'you mean?' he asked. 'What d'you mean by that?'

'Come with me,' she said, her voice weary.

They went back outside into the evening. The sky was breaking into blue and light, a little more with every moment. He followed her down the slopes below the house to the little cabin against the far wall. Suddenly she stopped and would go no further. He didn't go too close to her; somehow he felt he dared not.

'Just out of sight of their room,' she said, slow and bitter. 'That's where he used to take me, when he'd got rid of you to do something for him. That's where he used to take me, Somerled. And no one ever knew. I never breathed a word of it to anyone, because he told me I was his favourite, I was the best there was, and I was his happiness.'

Somerled looked now, and it was as though her face was covered in broken glass. The tears that coursed down her cheeks shone like broken glass in the evening light. He just stood there, aghast.

'I don't think she ever knew a thing. Or if she did she chose to ignore it, or just didn't care. She was too consumed with her own looks and preserving them, and with all her parties. Her bloody parties.'

He looked at the cabin and thought of the boat he had made there. It had been one place of sanctuary, because his mother had never known he was there. And he remembered her shouting, shouting from the front door. And how she would give up in the end and go back inside. He remembered just what that smile had felt like; he felt it now. But that two places could be so different, could carry such different air.

Now Deirdre hunched in real grief. He went forward and put his hands on her shoulders, but she shrank away, her hands clutching at her face.

'It's all right, I have to do this myself. You can't understand; this is something you simply can't. Go upstairs and I'll come and find you. Just give me time.'

He turned and went away, helpless. He had known nothing and so much made sense now, from the beginning. He climbed in the bathroom window and suddenly thought how nothing had changed. Even as adults they were coming back in the bathroom window because they couldn't come in the front door. And somehow it made sense; it made total sense.

He padded up the stairs as if he was afraid of being discovered. He was onto the upper landing far sooner than he expected; all of the place had compressed. But how often had he fallen up those stairs? And even when he had hurt himself and crouched there crying, his mother used to come out and tell him to be quiet, to for heaven's sake go up to his room more carefully.

What had happened to them? Where were they?

He went into his old bedroom. Of course none of it was the same; the estate had taken out all traces of the child's presence. But he saw it all as it had been nonetheless, and the world through the window was as it always had been. He rested his chin on the windowsill as he used to do when he was dreaming of his escape to Shuna. He would stay perfectly still so his mother could not chide him for some other noise, some other disturbance. And he would think how he was going to get the boat from the inlet, the boat with the sea urchins under it, and go out to Shuna for ever.

He knew suddenly that Deirdre was behind him in the doorway and didn't want to disturb him. And he felt so young; he felt so little changed. He was married now and would soon be bringing up his first child, and his own boyhood lay in this window and seemed still within reach. Had he learned nothing at all? Had he truly grown up?

'Do you want to go and see our mother?'

He didn't know how to answer; he didn't know what answer was possible. He turned round and looked at her – searching, questioning. The tears had gone from her face; the grief had not gone from her eyes.

'It's all right,' she said. 'There's no danger in it. It's not what you fear. All of that's gone and will never be again. Come on, it won't take long. We can walk round from the beach instead of going the whole way by the road.'

And so they crossed the top of the shore below the house, and there was no snow there at all. Almost no winter, just as there never had been when he wanted it most. Winter stopped at the road; it never came down to the house. It was just a bright, fierce wind that chased in over the water. It was cold so fingers could barely move any more. His face felt edged with ice; to speak was to chisel out words that sounded rough-hewn and incomplete.

At least the wind was behind them and the village ahead. He caught the rough, smoky scent of peat. They went in silence across the rubble of the boulders. He wanted to ask her things that he couldn't; it struck him that he knew nothing at all about her world. He wanted to know if she was happy; if she had found happiness after all this.

They came at last to the steps that led up beside the jetty. When they were growing up one fishing boat had gone out from here. If their mother was in a generous mood, she would give them a single coin on a Thursday afternoon to come running here to get prawns.

But where was Deirdre taking him? Their mother couldn't be here, in one of these houses that once had been built for the forestry workers. Then it came to him; the small care home at the top of the road, the one that was run by the church. Yet he still felt fear rising within him. What was he going to say?

Someone wheeled away from the entrance on a bicycle as they approached. It was warm inside – too warm – and there was a sweet smell, thick and cloying. A woman about Deirdre's age appeared, bright and smiling.

'Of course you can! It's a good time – she's just had supper and'll be up for another half-hour or so. Can I get you both a cup of tea?'

Deirdre turned to him and they both shook their heads. The woman led them down a corridor with a scuffed red linoleum floor. She tapped on the first door on the right and then went inside.

'That's two visitors for you, Diana! I'll see you later on!'

They went inside. She was sitting on a high-backed chair and smiled at them as soon as they came in. But the smile was as much a grimace as anything else, and she kept on repeating it after they sat down as though she was practising, as though this was something she was trying to perfect. She kept hold of their hands as they sat and he saw how painfully thin were her wrists; all of her head shrunk in on her shoulders, and the beautiful long straight hair of which she had been so desperately proud reduced now to a grey tangle.

'You see? She has no idea who we are and there would be no point telling her. All that world has gone, everything. So it's hard to be angry with her, because it's not her. She's gone.'

Suddenly she dropped Deirdre's hands and took Somerled's in both of hers and began stroking the back of it with the bones of her fingers. And she looked at him all the time, and the smile came and went, came and went. And he thought of all the times she could have held his hand and didn't. And he tried to feel pity for her and somehow thought it was too easy she should slip away like this and be exonerated. It was too easy. And he could bear it no longer and he pulled back his hand, and she took Deirdre's instead and fixed her gaze on Deirdre, smiling and not smiling, smiling and not smiling.

The woman who had met them suddenly came back. 'At least have a biscuit! Save us from ourselves!'

Politely they obliged and their mother ate one with an open mouth.

'So does she have many visitors?' Deirdre asked.

The woman shook her head very deliberately.

'Almost no one, I'm afraid. The minister comes to see everyone, of course. But, you see, she knows nobody. It's hard to know what to say, to know what she understands. So thank you for coming. Who are you?'

They told her. *I used to be her son*, he felt like saying. *Once upon a time, in a different world, I was her son. And she never loved me. Now she's sweet and holds my hand, and has no idea who I am. I don't know what to do with all the pain and anger; I've carried it in a sack for years until it's crippled me, and now I don't know what to do with it. I wanted to empty it in front of her, let her see the pain of it, and now there's no point. Now she's gone.*

Instead he said: 'I think it's time we were going. It's been a long day for both of us.'

And they got up and Deirdre was still talking to the woman. And he looked down at his mother and saw the crumbs of the biscuit around her mouth, and he thought of the parties she had had at the house. The friends there had been with their yachts and their cars and their jewellery. All the friends of whom she had been so proud. And now no one came to see her. And for a second, for the flicker of a second, he was glad. He was glad that she knew what it was to feel abandoned, to be forgotten, to be neglected. Then it passed. For she knew none of these things. This shadow below him was her ghost, no more than that. Suddenly he crouched down beside her and let her take his hand in hers.

'Goodbye then,' he said, and meant it.

It was getting dark and it was getting cold. The streetlights had come on, the yellow orange bleakness of them, and somehow it was the colour of what he felt inside. They walked up the road, fast.

'And what about our father?' he dared to ask.

'Oh, that's much easier. That won't take long at all.'

They went up to the top of the road, and instead of turning

back left towards the house and the hotel, she turned right. A hundred yards along the road was the church. He guessed where she was going.

CHARLES DANFORTH STEWART

There was something else on the headstone about his having been the beloved husband of Diana, and more below he couldn't read in the poverty of the light.

'There's our father,' she said. 'That's all that's left of him.'

And her voice was scarcely more than a whisper, and suddenly he remembered the day he finally cracked, had been able to take no more taunting about university and getting on in the world. He had gone and got his father's axe, his father's beloved axe, and brought it into the kitchen. And his mother had shrieked and he remembered his father's face perfectly, the thoughts that were working in his head. And as he talked he flexed the axe; he held it in his right hand and the left grasped the handle. And he talked for the first real time in his life. He opened the bottle of his rage and grief, and he poured it out in front of them. And what drove him half-mad was his mother's weeping, a weeping that was somehow composed of disappointment, a soft and simpering weeping that made no real tears. And he told them he was going and would never come back.

There was no more to say. He dared take a step closer to Deirdre and reach for her hand, half-afraid she would reject it. But she gripped it and suddenly she turned to him, her face wet, and he realised he was weeping himself. And he dropped the ghost of the axe from his right hand and they stood there together, crying out those years. For all of it was gone, all of it was dust. None of it existed any longer.

But then he thought of what she had had to carry, what she had been left with. Perhaps some kind of laying to rest of the years had been possible for him in the seeing of the ghost of his mother. But there was no father left for Deirdre to rage at. And he wondered if she had said or done anything before she too had left Davaar. He could not know and he could not ask. They were adults now and the rules were different.

It was so dark that even their father's name was invisible in the stone. And they cried no longer but just stood there, facing what they could not see. Then she let go of his hand, and they walked back to the road and the lights of the houses down below by the shore, and the way back to the hotel. And all that way they said nothing, for there was no more to be said.

The following day he woke early, before six. He had left the window open the night before and now he lay in the stillness and listened. The sound of the sea. No wind, nothing, just the wash of the sea on the shore. And then he got up, dressed soundlessly, and crept out into the grey fragments of the dawn. It hadn't frozen, but the air was raw and the tree branches hung still.

He reached the road and crossed it, half-ran to the top of their old drive. There he hesitated, unsure, hugging himself against the cold. Then he started down, fast, as far as the back of the house and then along the side of it. He went down over the lawns at the front, until he came to the little gate that clicked open and led to the shore. That sound had meant freedom; how many thousand times had it meant freedom? Through the long grass and out over the boulders that shrieked as his feet disturbed them. All the way down to the sea.

And then he made up his mind. He pulled off all his clothes and walked out, step by step, into the stone cold of that water. And he scrubbed himself violently until his legs and arms and neck felt red and raw. Then he pattered out, juddering with cold, and crouched until the freezing air had dried him. And he looked out at Shuna and thought that he no longer needed to go there. He thought of Anna and the house he had built and the House of the Sparrow, and he remembered that those were his refuges now; he needed no other.

At the hotel later he sat with Deirdre and had a breakfast the like of which he had not known before. There were clouds of warm rolls, and he was brought kippers that steamed, that tasted still of the sea. And they talked about the good things they remembered; the houses they visited at Hallowe'en, the croft where a pet pine marten was kept on a lead and ate honey and plums. And they laughed at things they had not thought of for long years. And he thought how glad he was he had found her friendship at last, that for all his parents had done they had not been able to prevent this.

But after breakfast a shadow came over her. Out in the lobby she said there were things she needed to do, that she needed time, and she kept looking away. He said he understood, he wanted to walk a while, and he wrapped up warm against the wind and went out. But at the bottom of the drive he wondered which way to go. He had forgotten so much, as though his memory had swept the years away because of the pain of them. He turned right as much to go in a different direction as anything else; it didn't matter where he went. He was still thinking about Deirdre, wondering what it was that she carried. He wondered if he would ever know her well enough that she would tell him, or that he would ask.

He turned a sharp corner and almost immediately a track led away steeply to the right, up the hill. Something flickered at the back of his mind; a tiny glimmer. He started up, though it was hard walking. There were deep craters of slush and mud, and the track went steeply and relentlessly into the wood. And then all at once a cottage on the left-hand side, made of timber, and the thud of an axe cutting logs. A tall man above the house, thin and grey, and the scent of pipe tobacco. He was looking across at the figure on the track.

'Somerled Stewart?'

Perhaps it was the sound of his voice that brought everything back. It was Donald, Donald Mackenzie, one of the estate men, and this was somewhere he used to come when he wasn't wanted at home. He'd stay there for hours on a Saturday, until Donald tired of him or feared the boy might be missed at Davaar and sent him packing. He went over now, through the last mud of the track, smiling, all of it coming back.

'Yes, it's me, Donald. It's me all right. I'm not staying long but I'll come in for a moment.'

And he stooped under the lintel and went into a room where he was fourteen years old. For nothing had changed, from the old chairs and rug to the open fire and clock, and even, it seemed, the Labrador that padded over to have a clap of his hand.

'Not Jess?'

The old man laughed. 'No, that's Jess's grandson. She's dead at least eight years. You've been gone too long! Now, you're having a dram.'

It might have been a question or a statement, but he knew it would have caused offence to argue. He heard Donald doing this and that in the tiny kitchen, telling him things and asking him things, the pipe always clamped in his mouth. He might have come out of the womb with that pipe. And finally he came through with a tray of tea and shortbread, and two glasses of whisky and a crystal jug of water.

'Donald, I'll not find the road again after all that whisky!'

'Then you're out of practice. It's not often I have visitors, and it's not often you come marching up my track. So here's to you. Now, tell me what brings you back and where it is that you've ended up. Because all of a sudden you were gone and we never heard any more of you.'

He talked about his father and home, how all of it had become too much for him and how he'd left, how he'd literally walked away.

'I understand,' Donald said, 'and none of that surprises me. But you should have come to say goodbye. I missed you. And Jess missed you too, I'll tell you! She never had walks like the ones she got from you!'

They laughed together and Donald thumped the side of the young dog that lay down again at the old man's feet and put his chin on his paws and sighed.

But Somerled realised that he meant it, that he had missed him, and that he should have said goodbye. And it touched him that he had been missed, for he had never thought of such a thing before.

'You know this; I think your father was envious of you.'

Somerled took a sip of whisky that burned down his throat. He looked at Donald, not understanding, not even beginning to know what he might mean.

'Your father's family were from here, Somerled – generations of them. Good Episcopalians that no doubt fought for the prince at Culloden. This place was very precious to him. But he'd been packed off to boarding school at God knows what age, sent to Edinburgh and an urban world. He came back here for his holidays, but that was it. Your father liked to talk about what he knew; whenever he was with the likes of me he tried to show off his knowledge, of places or people or whatever, but I think it was because he had to prove it to himself. Your mother didn't care, if you don't mind me saying so. Her head was too full of impressing the right people and keeping up with them. But your father actually wanted all that you had, and he couldn't get it. I think he was envious of the fact that you were having your childhood here, because his had been taken away from him. Now maybe I'm barking up the wrong tree, but I think there may be something in it.'

Somerled nodded. But he was thinking too about Deirdre, about what he'd discovered the day before. It haunted him. He had spent all those years believing he'd endured the worst of it; he had never the slightest thought that her world had been immeasurably more cruel.

'I took his axe from him!' he suddenly exclaimed, remembering how he had put it over his shoulder when he left.

'His father had inherited it; it was one of his most treasured possessions. That was why I did it.'

'Well, I hope at least you've used it since.'

And he told Donald about all of his new world, about the building of the House of the Sparrow first. For it had been Donald who had first taught him how to hold an axe, here behind this very house. And he told him about the carving he was doing now, all the mundane and everyday woodwork, but the real carving too. And he wished he had put the wren or the otter in his pocket before he came away from the hotel, for it would have been good to show the old man. It would have been a moment of pride, but somehow a thanking too. For it was Donald who had first set him off on the journey.

'Would you come and see us, Donald?' he asked suddenly, shyly.

The old man laughed as he got up to put another log on the fire, the pipe still clamped in his jaws. 'Not a chance of it,' he said. 'I've hardly left the house in three years, and that was to go as far as the village to visit. No, my days for journeys are done. One can journey in the mind, Somerled. You've told me all about the place you've built, and you've given me a picture. And that'll come back to me many times.'

The boy nodded, for he felt a boy again here. Suddenly he felt something rise within him and he went over and crouched in front of the old man and his dog, and he gripped his hand. 'Thanks for all you gave me when I was growing up here, Donald. Not just knowledge, but kindness. I had precious little of that at home and I always had kindness here. Thank you for it.'

The old man chuckled as he got up, but his eyes were glinting. 'I'd better go out with you and see about another log or two for the fire. Now you take care and send my love to that young wife of yours. And I hope everything goes well with the birth when it comes.'

And Somerled thanked him and watched him all the time as he went, for he knew there was precious little chance he would see him again. And he walked down the track remembering how it was to go home back then and how little he ever wanted to go at all. And he realised they had mentioned Deirdre not once, and he remembered that he had never wanted to bring Deirdre here or for her to find out too much about it. This was his place, his place alone.

He walked down to the bottom of the track, his trousers spattered with slush and mud, and he stopped. He had dreaded coming here because he hadn't known what to say, and he had found the words. It had been worth it; all of it. But it was Deirdre who had had the greater courage in facing it.

When he got back to the hotel he found her reading in front of the open fire. The Germans were getting ready to go out hunting; the lobby was loud with shouting and laughter. He could tell by Deirdre's face that something had happened; she was pale and drawn, distant. She told him she would have to leave early the next morning; that she would be met at the hotel at ten. He nodded, not wanting to remind her that he would have to be met too, that he would be travelling with her. It seemed petty and he only nodded. He had carried back with him the goodness of his hour with Donald; he did not want it lost. He almost told her it had happened, but she had returned to her book and it was as though a door had been closed. A door he did not dare disturb.

There was light on the furthest hills and he wished he could be on them. It brought back memories of being forbidden to go out on a Saturday or Sunday because there was piano practice to be done or his room to tidy. He would see the light outside and fear that by the time he had finished it would be too late and it would have gone. And sometimes in winter that was exactly what happened; by three the sun had dropped like a ball of ice behind the hills and the skies sank into deep, dark blue. He thought about what Donald had said about his father's envy and he wondered if that really had been the case. He had always wondered why he hadn't been sent off to private school in Edinburgh like his father. In fact he wondered why both he and Deirdre hadn't gone; he knew that money had been no issue. And then suddenly he thought of Deirdre and what she had endured here, and how almost none of that would have been possible had she been in Edinburgh. Perhaps it was that that had kept him here in the end too.

He went out in the afternoon, back down to the village. And he saw something he had not noticed the previous night in the darkness – a telephone box. And he thought of Anna and wished he could call, but he had not a coin in his pocket. He thought for a moment of going back to the hotel to ask Deirdre, but it would have seemed pathetic somehow. He would be home the following day.

He went instead into the little church, through its unlocked door. There were some flowers in the porch whose petals must have fallen months before. He closed the door behind him, gently, as though coming in late to a service. They had been here irregularly over the years; when there were big yachting events or parties, church was conveniently forgotten. If nothing else was happening, it was an important occasion. He saw his mother putting her face on at the dressing-table in their bedroom. He was wearing a kilt and he had to stand behind her and turn around so she could look at him in the mirror. There was always something wrong: a garter, a sock, his hair. If she could find nothing wrong she said nothing, went back to her own reflection and left him waiting till he just went away.

His father had been a great singer of church hymns. He had a good voice; how many times had the organist begged him to join the little choir? But it would have been too much of a commitment, Somerled thought now. It would have demanded too much sacrifice.

He went deeper into the church, towards the altar. To the left, the stained-glass window of the Good Shepherd. This was where they always sat on the Sundays they were here, with their backs to that window. *Suffer the little children to come unto me.*

He thought how the words were so often misunderstood now. And yet he thought of Deirdre and himself too, and the bitter irony of the misunderstanding. At fourteen she had announced she didn't believe in God any more and would no longer be made to go to church.

'But, Deirdre,' her mother had said when they got home, 'it doesn't matter whether you believe in God or not. It's important that you're there!'

As though that made perfect sense and required no post-script. What she really meant, of course, was that she was *seen* to be there. Deirdre was still made to join them whenever the family attended, but now she refused to sing any of the hymns. As her father sang beside her, his fine tenor voice filling the church, she stood beside him with her arms folded. She almost managed not to be confirmed, but in the end the lure of the presents and the party was too much for her.

He thought of the church in the glen and its minister. He was not sure that he believed, but he believed in the minister's belief. The man lived it, no matter what the cost. He would go to see a dying man at five in the morning, and he sought no praise for his journey. Perhaps one day Somerled would tell him something of all this. He would listen and understand; of that Somerled felt sure.

Would he bring his child here? Would he bring Anna here? He was not sure what there was left to show them but the broken fragments of all that had been. It made sense to him because the umbilical cord remained; emotions were buried in whichever direction he turned. All he could tell them were old stories.

He closed the door as quietly as he had opened it and started back up the road. Snow was falling; not whole flakes but the tiniest fragments. He lifted his face and the fingers of the air brushed his cheeks and eyes and mouth. And he found himself smiling, for it was teasing and healing and gentle. And he thought of Anna. Everything happened so fast the following day. All his exchanges with Deirdre were over practical things; what time he would meet the train and where he would wait if need be. He thanked her again for his stay at the hotel and she brushed aside his words as if they were an annoyance. Everything seemed an annoyance but it was as if he could see the pain she carried, as though it was a visible weight.

Murdo was suddenly there and they were outside under

thick grey skies. There had been nothing more than a breath of snow overnight and the road was clear enough. What a different journey it was. Now almost not a word was exchanged; Murdo chewed on something all the time and asked not a thing about their days. Deirdre seemed hunched in her seat, hunched and clenched as if she was facing something that lay ahead, something invisible. The only thing Murdo asked in the end was if he was sure he didn't want a lift to Inverness. He might be there several hours quicker and there was room and plenty for him in the car. Deirdre said nothing. He thanked Murdo but said that he had a return ticket and had one or two things he should do in the town. He wasn't sure what things but those were the words that came to him. And then he got out into the quiet of the place, and thanked them for the lift and told them not to bother getting out into the cold to say goodbye, and the car hummed away.

He spoke to no one until he came to Pitnacraig. But it was good to have those hours, especially on the first train through the nowheres of the west, the only sound the *ta-tara, ta-tara* of the train on the tracks. He thought about everything he had seen and everything that had come back to him, and he knew that he was glad he had gone there. He would not have done it alone; he would not have thought of making the journey. How much he would have to tell Anna when he came home. The man he spoke to when he got off the train in Pitnacraig was handing out religious pamphlets. He was an old man, so desperately thin and frail. Somerled feared that a puff of wind would send him over the platform edge onto the lines. His cheeks were sunken and the blue veins stood out on his hands and wrists as he tried to separate one of the pamphlets from the rest. Yet Somerled waited to take one as others walked away, and the grace of the smile the old man gave him when finally he had found a single pamphlet was quite beautiful. And all the man said was *God bless you*, and his voice was as soft as a bird's. And Somerled thanked him as he left the freezing wind of the platform and went to catch the bus home. Yet he couldn't forget him. He wondered what the man lived from, and he wondered too at the devotion that made him stand there waiting for trains on such a day.

And when he got off the bus in the village, into at least an inch of new snow, the first person he saw was Allan. And in his joy he ran to try to catch up with him, and he shouted his name, but he was perhaps too far ahead and never heard him. He was wheeling a barrow and walking even more briskly than usual, his arms bare in all that cold.

Somerled's heart sang to be back and he could have danced for joy. Here was everything he loved.

As he careered up the track, skidding on frozen stones, he suddenly wondered if Anna might be staying with her parents. Yet somehow he felt sure she was not, that she was in the glen. Ahead of him in the west, a white sun was about to flicker its last cold light in the high hills that ringed them. Their tops were honey-gold, and he wished that one day he might stand in such a moment of light, seeing the shadow that lay all around.

He came red and breathless to the door, went in and closed it, dropped his bags in the hallway. He stood panting, listening to the house, and then went into the room with the fire to be assaulted by the warmth. And there was Anna, sitting there, her face white and one hand up at her mouth. She stared at the flames. He went down beside her and tried to take her hand.

'It was worth doing. I saw my mother, though she's past recognising anyone. And Deirdre took me to where my father's buried in the churchyard. But it was more than that. It was about going back there and facing all of it. And I met someone I knew through all the hardest years! And – a place in Inverness wants to take my carvings, my good carvings! Isn't that wonderful?'

But all that time she had not looked at him, and long before the end of what he said he knew she was not happy. And he tried to make her look at him and she would not, and he tried again, he tried to pull her hand away from her face and she began weeping. And his heart thudded and he was wordless; he asked her then over and over what was wrong. He begged to know what was wrong and what he had done, for he was sure it must be what he had done.

But all at once she got up, quickly, and went away to their own room and closed the door behind her. And he heard the pulse of his heart and the fire's voice as its yellow-white heart crackled and sputtered. He sat there until he could stand it no longer and he got up and went to their room, paused, then opened the door soundlessly to find her.

She did not turn away from him now. She lay there, her face on the pillows, her eyes red holes that had wept themselves out. She stared from them, not blinking, with an emptiness that haunted him. He tried to hold her, to say fragments of things, brush the hair from her eyes. But she only stared, until in the end he turned away himself. He had no more to say or offer, and he did not know what it was that he had done. All that he had come home with seemed washed away.

And then suddenly she rose and leaned over him, and her red eyes met his. They searched him and he half-turned beneath her.

'All this time I was here on my own,' she said, her voice soft, almost no more than a whisper. 'You left me here, Somerled, and I might still lose my baby; we've not passed the time of danger yet.'

He was about to speak, to explain, and he tried to rise up in the bed, but she wasn't done. She kept him where he was, went on.

'But it's more than that, Somerled. I thought a lot when you were gone; I didn't go to stay with my parents at all in the end. I felt I needed to be here, that it was right I was here. But I thought about how little you really know me. I know you love me, and you show me you love me, but I don't think you know me at all. What makes me afraid; where I've come from; what's really in my mind. Maybe I don't know you well enough either, maybe you would tell me that.'

Now he struggled to sit up, to muster his own thoughts. 'And I think about how little you know my world!' he said indignantly. 'I'm glad I went over with Deirdre because I'd never have had the courage to go alone. Neither of us was loved; we had parents too busy with boats and dogs and parties to care about their children. My father used to tell me he was sick of the sight of me. Can you imagine growing up feeling you're unwanted every day? When I left to come here I ran away; I left it all behind because I simply couldn't face it any more. I left because I was afraid I'd kill my father, and I think there were times I really might have done it. I came here to begin again, to find myself. And you helped me do it.'

The grief gathered in him and she reached out and rocked him, her head against his shoulder. Then in the end she looked straight at him.

'We have to be good to each other,' she said. 'Soon we'll have a child and everything will be turned upside down. Everything will change after he's arrived.' She stroked his hair.

'After she's arrived,' he said.

'No,' she smiled. 'He.'

'I'm sure it's a girl,' he said softly, and there was a trace of a smile at the corners of his lips too, but he meant it all the same.

'And I'm sure it's going to be a boy,' she told him.

She was going to get up and he held her back.

'I can work with an axe and a plane; I'm learning how to make beautiful things. But what you want is harder. I'm not good at finding words, at weighing them or shaping them so they're right. I'd rather work with wood than words. And maybe that has to do with growing up. My father never wanted to talk to me, unless it was to give me some task to do, unless it was a way of getting rid of me from the house for an hour or two. I grew used to my own company; I had to. I spent hours by myself on the beach, searching for things – searching and searching. I didn't mind silence; it was better than being in an unhappy house. What I'm trying to say, Anna, is that you have to help me. You have to be patient with me. I can't just change like that into what you want me to be. It takes time to learn.'

She nodded and suddenly he broke into a grin, leaned forward and held her and rolled her over onto her back.

'But you're wrong about one thing! I'm telling you we're having a girl!'

And she laughed and tried to escape, and he held her and they lay there for a time, not talking, and when they looked up again it was snowing. Great big flakes twirling out of the sky like dancers, and the silence they fell from so huge, so incomprehensibly huge.

'Well, whether it's a boy or girl,' Anna said, looking up, 'you have to make a sledge for them!'

And he nodded. He remembered being back in the garden and on the shore where he had grown up, and how he had yearned for the snow to fall just once. Here, inland among the hills, it never seemed to stop.

But it was not just a sledge that he worked on in those next days in the House of the Sparrow, it was a bear. For in one of the long pieces of bogwood he had found on the shores of the bigger loch, there was the figure of a bear, up and rearing, its mouth in mid-roar. He saw it and felt it and knew he had to find it. His fingers and mind trembled with the hunt for it, and three days later he was almost done with the last work on the mouth when Anna came in. He looked up, startled.

'Did you not hear me?' she said, her voice tired and cold.

He looked at her, still coming out of his world, his place.

'Hear you?' he repeated foolishly, as though the words made no sense.

'I called you for supper half an hour ago and you answered,' she said, and now her voice rose in real anger and frustration at him. 'And here you are labouring over a carving that won't sell, and we have baby clothes to buy and any amount to save for! And you disappear for three days and can't think of anything but this when you're back in the house. Why did you bother marrying at all, Somerled? You'd have been happier here on your own without a wife and baby disturbing you!'

And she turned and had gone down the path before he had the presence of mind to call her back, though he wondered later if she would have stopped even if he had. And he turned the bear in his hands, in the near-darkness of the evening. He had wanted to carve new things for the shop in Inverness; he wanted them to be the best he had ever made, and his hands were full of urgency. He sat there a few moments, frozen, like a carving himself, and all of what she had said echoed in his head. Then he went down at last to the house, opened the door tentatively, almost as though not wanting to disturb. The table was set for the two of them but she was not there. And from their room he heard the long, low sound of her crying. But he did not dare go in, for some reason he did not dare. And when he ate he found he could barely swallow the food; it felt too dry in his throat and he did not taste it. And all the time he sat there he heard her crying, and he wondered at everything, and thought again of all that he had wanted this place to be. And he wondered if it was a dream, something that could only ever be a fantasy, a perfect place in the imagination. And was that not always the way of things?

And in his mind he went back to Davaar, for that had been his father's place, and however many generations of Stewarts before him. He had inherited the house and he had met the beauty, Diana Temple, when she was up on holiday with her parents. They had a yacht they kept in Oban, and they were sailing the west coast that summer. She had never gone home; they married before the year was out. Had his father dreamed of their days at Davaar as he had done of those here in the glen? It was hard to think unlikely, and perhaps in the beginning it had been like that, before either Deirdre or he had been born. Perhaps it had been a kind of Eden.

Still he heard the long, slow sadness of Anna's crying and still he could not go in and face her, and it angered him. He had been working hard; that was all he had been doing. Was he to be blamed for that? Would she have him slave at things that were to sell for a few pence day in and day out? Was he never allowed to consider himself a craftsman? He got up and went over to the kitchen window. And slowly he realised he was looking at lights and hearing voices. He was roused out of his stupor and ran to get his coat. He went out the front door and slammed it behind him, and the night was billowing snowflakes so he hardly saw the way in front of him. And he slid and fell and twisted his ankle. Pain shot through his leg and he struggled upright, limped on down the hill. He was furious with himself, for falling out with Anna, with this.

And suddenly in front of him were three men and a woman with horses. All talking; the wind full of talk and snow and the warmth of the horses' breath. He found it hard to speak because of the pain. And a torch they were flashing about hurt his eyes.

'What the devil are you doing up here tonight?'

A big hand came down on his shoulder and a face loomed close to his. The mouth was sour with the stink of whisky and he wanted to turn away. He felt sick with it, sick and angry.

'Fellow Stewarts! Heading up the glen and through to the

west. We're meeting Stewarts from there tomorrow night or the following day. So you'll let us stay here the night?'

Somerled shook the hand off his shoulder and twisted away from the mouth. They were unloading things; ready to move in before he'd even had time to think! He'd known plenty of travellers when he was growing up; he might even have been familiar with the ones they said they were off to meet in the west. He remembered how his mother had detested all of them; hated that the name Stewart she had earned from her husband should be confused with this shameful branch of layabouts.

'No!' he found himself shouting. And everything of that night was in his voice: the pointless quarrel with Anna, the night's snow and his fall, perhaps even the tiny thumb-print of his mother's snobbery.

'No! You damned well cannot!' And he found himself fighting with the other man as he brought something from his horse. He was beside himself with rage and pain, beyond thinking straight, and the two fellows, twice his strength and more, knocked him back into the snow. He cleared his mouth of snow.

'You can stay here when you find the manners to ask!' he shouted, struggling to get up and maddened with the pain in his ankle. 'The world doesn't owe you lodgings and it's time you got that!'

The other man pulled him up out of the snow by the lapels of his jacket. There was no smell of whisky from him. Somerled saw him draw back his hand and waited for the blow, but none came. The face turned away a moment but the hands still held him.

'Jess, tell him something he doesn't want to hear!'

He was silent now and shivering, more aware of the pain than of anything else. He had no more words in him; he had said his piece. He was propped up between the three of them like a puppet whose strings have snapped. And the woman looked at him and she was beautiful. Her eyes were wide-spaced and dark, her face long and the cheekbones high. Even with all this churning inside him he was aware of her beauty. He thought in that second he had never seen any woman so beautiful in all his life.

'You have a wife who's going to have a child,' she said, and he heard the sadness in her voice. He saw the dark sadness in her eyes and he heard it also in her voice. 'And that child will be full of shadow,' she said, and a chill passed through him, and afterwards he thought about how she had spoken those words, and wondered whether they were a statement or a threat or a warning.

And as though in a dream and in slow motion they gathered their last things and threw them onto the cart and looked at him, and turned west and began that way, the snow billowing against them. And he fell backwards, useless, into the snow, and his hand struck the edge of a rock. And he looked away and swore, over and over again, at his useless folly and at the pain that gnawed at his ankle and now at his hand. And then at last he heard his name being called from the house and he roared back that he was coming, and he staggered up the hill.

Anna put his foot in a basin of warm water and saw to his cut hand. She brought him a dram of whisky even though he told her he didn't want it, and she poured it into a mug of scalding hot tea that tasted tarry and thick. All of it she did in silence, and he grumbled like a five-year-old there, dishevelled and foolish, in front of the fire. But all of it was fear; fear for what had happened, fear for what had been said. He didn't dare tell her they were travellers who had wanted shelter for the night; travellers he had shouted at and refused permission to stay. He dared tell her nothing of it at all.

They slept together that night, except that they did not. They each hugged their corner of the darkness, and he did not know if she slept as he lay awake, wide awake, listening to the wind and snow. And he thought of the travellers and could not get them from his mind; he feared that night that he would never forget them as long as he lived. For the anger he had felt was gone; all the stupidity of that moment had flooded away like the water of high tide from a cave. It was replaced by grief and fear, and they ate at him in the darkness. He slept in the end, was washed into a kind of rest, but he woke again about five and remembered everything and felt tired beyond words. He turned and reached out to hold Anna, and then knew that he could not touch her. She lay as she had done all those hours before, and he did not know if she had slept or if she lay awake still, listening and waiting. And once he almost reached out to pull her round to him, to tell her what he had done, to tell her everything and beg her forgiveness. But even as he reached out he doubted; the words failed him and fell away, and he turned once more into the shell of his own darkness.

She said no more about the previous night, but then they spoke about precious little. He dared not even look at the carving of the bear but spent the whole day churning out all the things he knew would sell and were wanted. He did it as though to please her and yet never once did she come up to the House of the Sparrow. He looked out for her, anxious and hoping, but she never came. He went down to dinner in the end, his heart loud and his hands foolish, and they talked about fragments of nothing, distant from each other and measured and careful.

'I'm going to stay with my parents this weekend,' she said, lifting something to a cupboard as she spoke. 'There's new soup made and there should be enough apart from that to eat. And I'll be back before it's dark on Sunday.'

He wanted to get up from the table and turn her round, take her face in his hands and tell her he was sorry. But instead he sat there, stupid, eating and barely tasting what he ate.

And after a whole morning of work he came down to the house and opened the door and knew as he went inside that she had gone. He called her name and he heard the forlornness in his own voice. His feet moved on the wood and there was silence; outside a chaffinch looked at him, its head on one side and then the other, and he saw that the feeder was empty. She had not come to say goodbye. It was that which lingered with him, that he could not forget all the long day.

He had a box full of carvings and he knew there was neither need nor point in doing any more. The last work that required doing on the bear took the merest blink of an eye, but then he got out the biggest and the best piece of bogwood he had found, and started work on what he thought was a hidden fox. But he realised as he carved that he had the head all wrong, and he looked at the wood and knew it was wasted. He threw it to the floor in fury and put his head in his hands. There was no point carving when his mind was elsewhere.

His whole being had to be focused on the finding; if it wasn't, it was nothing more than wasted time.

Outside his shed, that first place he had built with his own hands however long ago, it was a nothing day. The temperature hovered around zero; the ground was neither crisp with frost nor did the snow melt. And the skies hung low and grey, a strange orange to them, and there was not a breath of wind. He went a little later to do no more than stand in the silence of the yard, and he heard the voices of two ravens flapping west. It was as though they went through a kind of water, and it came to him that perhaps the sky was to birds as the sea for fish. And they headed west until he could follow them no further, and he remembered that last day he visited the loch and went out to the island frozen at its heart, and how he had looked to the top of the glen, beyond the waterfall and its gold. And he thought again how one day he must go there.

At least he had boxed up his best carvings to send to Inverness before the day was done. He laboured over a letter; wrote it half a dozen times before he was content with it, and even then he still wished that Anna had been there to tell him it was good enough to send. And then, all of a sudden, he remembered what she'd said about a sledge, that whether it was to be a boy or a girl there had to be a sledge.

He went and rooted about in his boxes and found nothing that would do, nothing that seemed just right. It had to be new wood, he thought. And he went and got out the axe, and as he crouched there in the shadows he saw the blade of it gleam. And he shivered as he picked up the handle; he thought of the hands that had held it, and he remembered how proud his father had been of it. This, in a strange way, had been his inheritance. And like the Prodigal Son, he had taken his inheritance before time and gone off with it. And yet he had not gone back home again; there had been no going back to beg forgiveness. He had taken his inheritance and he had not turned round. And he thought of Deirdre; all of what she had told him flashed across his mind, and he felt neither shame nor remorse. For what should he have asked forgiveness?

He went up to the wood behind the house, the wood that lay below the top of the ridge. He went fast, the axe over his shoulder and his breath clouding the air. And though he had no idea why, he felt the better for going there, for being there. The wood was sparse; between the dwarf pines and rowans were round boulders covered now in deep mounds of snow. A flock of little birds passed through a moment after he got there; they flew low, flickers of red visible on their backs. And then his foot moved on a boulder and they were gone, all of them, in a single breath.

He chose a tree with a thick trunk. He set to work with the axe and he wondered just how far the sound of it travelled that day, in the hugeness of the silence.

After he had brought it down he worked to clear away the branches from its sides. The blade of the axe cut fine and clean; the sweet scent of the resin came to his nostrils, it clouded the air all around. But he realised it wasn't enough, that he'd need a second trunk. His eyes scanned the trees and he saw another pine twenty or thirty yards higher up.

He was going there, his mind on nothing else, when he found the stag. It lay there in front of him, almost a part of the land itself. There was a thin covering of snow on its flank, on all of it, so it was somehow rendered ghostly, otherworldly. Its head was twisted and its mouth was open, as though it was for ever in mid-roar. And as he crouched there he wondered what had happened to bring it down. Had it fallen perhaps on the icy rocks, fallen and died of exposure here among the rocks? And it made Somerled think somehow of how great things fall, of how nothing is too great to fall. And it was both a comfort and a shadow.

He went back to the House of the Sparrow with two thick trunks of pine. He returned with the axe first, didn't risk leaving it to pick up later. It was too precious for that; it meant far more to him than the mere value of its smooth handle and sharp blade. Then he came back for the trunks and he dragged them behind him. He stopped often, out of breath, and they snagged on things and got half-buried in ditches. He returned to the house in a lather of sweat and he washed and ate, dried himself in front of the bright flames of the living-room fire. Then, just as it was starting to get dark once more about four o'clock, he went back out to begin work. He was more himself now, he knew; he had ceased to think only of Anna, to tumble around in his head the whole confusion of their quarrel. His hands no longer trembled with it.

He cut the trunks into the pieces of wood he wanted. He set about shaping and smoothing them, and he relished the scent of them there in the cabin. He had set out all the lamps he could find, for he had no electric light in the House of the Sparrow. That would come one day, if the money were ever to be found. The place was filled with a honey-yellow light he loved, and the work warmed him. All at once he knew how the pieces of the sledge must fit together and his whole hands filled with purpose. It was as though they moved of their own volition. He was somehow beyond thinking; his actions were not planned any longer, they were not cerebral. They became instinctive, and once he reached that point he knew he would make no mistakes. There was no arrogance in the realisation, and it was not conscious thought – it was knowledge.

So he worked till he was done. When he looked up, finished, he was still crouching on the floor of the cabin. Two of the candles had burned out completely. He looked at them and tried to think how many hours' burning had been in them. He got up, dizzy, and he saw that one of his hands was bleeding. A deep red trail disappeared through the yellow stain of the wood. All at once he realised just how cold it was, and he shuddered with it. He put out the lights and went down to the house. Only his hands and eyes were tired but he went to bed all the same. And he slept sound, for he knew that he had found something.

He was asleep too when Anna came back that Sunday afternoon. She found him there in the House of the Sparrow; on one side of the table was the sledge, and it shone in the last gold of the day's light. She ran her finger along one of the runners, and a smile touched her lips, yet there was a sadness in it also. On the other side was a pine marten he had found in a piece of bogwood. All but the breast was dark, the colour of rich chocolate, but the tummy was golden-yellow. He had even caught the glitter of the beast's eyes. She picked it up and turned it in her hand, looking at that head, and she wondered just how many hours he had slaved at it.

She had told her parents her news at last. There had been neighbours in the house and there had been songs and the playing of fiddles. No one was in their bed before two that morning, yet there in the darkness it had been Somerled she missed. For he should have been with her and was not. And then as now, in the House of the Sparrow, she did not know how to reach him. It was just like this, as though one of them was awake and the other slept.

He did things to please her that evening: he set the table and made a fire that thundered in the chimney. He kept asking her if she needed things and hovered around her. She knew she should feel gratitude and yet she wanted him to stop. She told him to leave her be, that she was no invalid and that he'd done enough. He crouched in front of the fire and she wanted to go and hold him; she watched him out of the corner of her eye and she did nothing.

He was thinking about the travellers and what the woman had said. He saw her face endlessly in front of his, and her words echoed and echoed until he was driven half-mad by them. He tried to tell himself that if the whole story were to come out now he would make it far bigger than ever it had been to begin with. Yet it haunted him and he wanted it gone; it would come to him that he would never be happy again unless he made his confession.

'My mother's not well,' she murmured at supper, and blew on the soup she had made. 'She has pain in her side and she'll do nothing about it. It was my father that told me; she would say nothing.'

He became anxious and asked how long she had had it and if there was anything else that was wrong with her and if Allan would manage to persuade her in the end to see a doctor.

She clattered her spoon in the empty bowl and scraped back her chair. 'I don't know, and I had no idea you'd become so concerned about my mother.'

He sat with his own empty bowl as she went for the next course.

'I'm sorry,' she said when she came back. 'I'm tired, and we hardly parted on the best of terms. And yes, I'm worried, though I have no answer to my worries. My mother won't go near a doctor.'

'Did you see the sledge?' he asked shyly, remembering it.

'Yes, I did – it's fine.'

'Would you have said nothing if I hadn't asked?' he said quietly, but the bitterness was there. He looked away at his food, feeling her eyes on him as she sat down.

'It wasn't uppermost on my mind, no, but neither did I ignore it. Is carving the only thing left in your head? Is that all you can do?'

'I worked on that sledge all through the night,' he said. 'And I was proud to make it. The labour of my hands is the best thing I have to give!'

'Then work on other things too!' she said, so quietly it was all but a whisper. And he shook his head as he ate fast, for he didn't know what more to say. He felt like weeping and could not weep. And he envied her ability to cry so easily, for no matter how right he felt it was her weeping that always silenced and confused him. And he would have wept now but he knew no tears would come.

He got up early that Monday, long before dawn had

properly come. He neither ate nor drank anything, but picked up the parcel that was ready to begin its journey to Inverness and started down the track. He found himself thinking he was back on the west coast, at Davaar, and the sadness of that suddenly flooded him. After all he had built, and after Anna, could he really yearn for that place? What was there truly that he missed? What could there be to miss, either now or then?

The schoolchildren were gathering to meet the bus when he arrived. Their child would one day take the same bus on the same journey. If they still lived in the house in the glen. It was the first time he had allowed himself to think such words. In two weeks' time it would be Christmas.

He had been headed for the post office but for some reason he turned instead to the blacksmith's to find Allan. The place was as it always was on a Monday: the same scents and sounds and labour. And Allan just as ever; the same wide smile that filled his face. He held out his huge blackened hand to shake Somerled's own.

'Time? There's always time if I stop to look for it, and it's an excuse for tea! We started at four this morning and I haven't stopped since then. And how are you both, or all three of you!'

He lied of course, or he said at least that they were fine. But then he found himself talking all the same about the travellers and that night they had passed the house on their way up the glen. And he told no less than everything; it was a kind of confession, for all of it lay buried in him still. The fear of what he had done, of what he had not done.

And Allan burst out laughing when he was done and rubbed his eyes. 'Somerled, I've known those three since they were playing in the river! The only time they're to be feared is when they stagger out of an alehouse on a Saturday night. I know horses that have more sense of the future than them. What you did is no less than what all of us have done – you lost your temper. It was a late end to a long day. They were only trying to frighten you and they succeeded. They must have known from someone here – perhaps even from me! – that Anna was expecting a child. There's no more to it than that. Now let it go and never trouble Anna with a bit of it. You'll make more of it by talking than you will by leaving it behind.'

But he told Allan too about something of their unhappiness. He found himself shy of the words; this was his father-in-law and it felt awkward. But he chose him because he was Anna's father, because he knew her and might help him find a road back. He didn't make big of it; he had no wish for the man to think after this short time they had all but given up. And what he did convey was confused; he struggled for words like a man out of his depth in the sea. And the more he felt a fool the more he sensed he behaved like one. But in the end Allan laid that huge hand against his upper arm.

'She's making her nest, Somerled. I remember enough of those years when Martha and I were settling in the village. All of it began like magic; we were dizzy with each other, couldn't wait to come home to talk and be together. Then came the children.'

And he laughed; he leaned back his head and laughed. 'That sorted us out all right. I don't think we fought a single time before then, and that first baby was the hardest. Everything changes, Somerled – everything. All that you think you knew. And it's worst for the women. They don't know what's hit them. But their need to prepare for and protect that child is everything. We just stumble along behind. So be good to her; be as good to her as you can be and be patient. Martha and I'll do the best we can to help, though Martha's not as well as she should be.'

And Somerled heard his voice break; he almost felt the jolt that passed through him, that big bear of a man, who looked as though nothing in this world would ever rock him, far less topple him. And Somerled saw that his eyes were glassy and looked away. Allan had been going to say more, Somerled was certain, but he didn't. Instead he got back on his feet.

'I need to keep working, forgive me. But I'm glad you came to talk, and come back whenever you need or want to.' And he held out his hand once more and the eyes still sparkled.

'Send Martha my love,' Somerled said lamely, and he turned and went out into the morning. The school bus had gone and a straggle of geese was passing low over the roofs, and he looked up and watched them. They were starving, poor things, he thought, and all at once it put him in mind of the travellers and that night.

He went across the street to the post office and he felt the tremble of his hands. George was parcelling up something for one of the estates as he went in; the woman was standing there in her tweeds and headscarf.

'I'd have sent Ellie in with it herself, George, but I wanted to make sure about delivery dates for Christmas. These are very dear friends of ours in London, and it's imperative they have the pheasants for a dinner party on the seventeenth. Now, can you guarantee they'll be there for then?'

The woman took off her half-moon glasses at that point, as

though holding them in her right hand as she leaned on the counter somehow gave more weight to her argument.

George was busy with the brown tape – acres of it, just as requested. He was the same to everyone: jovial, twinkling, unhurried. He looked at her and shrugged his shoulders.

Barring acts of God and war, the pheasants would arrive in London on time. Maybe if she had let them fly there of their own accord it would have been quicker, that was all he could say. The attempt at humour was lost on Lady Olivia who reluctantly accepted there was no more she could do and strutted out.

But before Somerled could hand over the parcel to George, the postmaster had pointed at him. 'That fellow Neil was in here only ten minutes ago looking for you! Now let me think where he said he was going. I can't for the life of me remember, Somerled, I'm so sorry. But he was anxious to find you, that's for sure.'

George had come out from behind the glass partition to stand beside Somerled. He was looking up and down the street as though somehow that would help the man to materialise.

'You mean the Neil who knows my sister?'

George nodded at him as though that should have been established a long time ago. 'And there he is!' he exclaimed, and he leaped at the door and had it open and jingling in a second. Somerled was behind him and saw the figure coming over. He was somehow younger than he'd imagined he might be; all muffled up against the cold. His piercing dark eyes met Somerled's and he held out his hand to him as George chattered his introductions.

'Let's go and talk at the inn,' he said quietly. 'Thank you, George.'

The fellow had no wish to talk before they got there. Somerled said something lame about the winter and the length of it, and the fellow made no attempt to respond. He just walked fast and stayed hunched in his long coat and thick scarf, pushing forward all the time.

There was no one inside when they got there and it was clear they expected no one. The fire was a small orange glow in the corner and the rest of the place was dark and cold. The man chose a table at once, as far away from the bar as possible, and about as far from the warmth too. Somerled asked for tea in a half-whisper. He went back to the table smiling, taking off his coat and smiling all the time.

'Deirdre is dead,' the man called Neil said, not looking at him, looking down at the table in front of him. Somerled gasped but said nothing, only watched, frozen, waiting.

'You know that her face was burned,' Neil said. Only now did he look up.

Somerled nodded dumbly. Of course he knew; of course he had seen.

The tea came and the cups and saucers rattled on the wooden surface of the table. Hugh, the one who'd come with the tray, prattled about the cold of the place, apologising for the fire and the lack of light. He grinned and talked endlessly and aimlessly, and Somerled wished him away; he wanted to know; he had to know. He felt dizzy. Deirdre dead. How was it possible? How in all the world was it possible?

'Let me tell you from the beginning,' Neil said, once Hugh

had finally gone. He leaned in to the table, as he had leaned in to the cold outside.

'Deirdre was married to a man from Ireland. She wasn't married to him for long, but they were married. It was he who burned her face.'

Somerled looked at him incredulous.

'He had come from Ireland in great poverty and had settled somewhere close to Glasgow. Eventually he moved north and that's when he met your sister. He was still poor and he was depressed, and I think your sister believed she could help him. She always believed she could help him. He was grateful – most of the time he was gentle, the kindest man you could meet – but he had these blind rages and he was strong, ferociously strong. And I think Deirdre persisted in her belief that she could heal him. Yes, I think the word heal is best. I really think she thought that in the end she could do it. Perhaps she even tried to persuade him of that too, I don't know. But four days ago he killed her.'

'What happened?' Somerled asked. He had folded in on himself; he felt like a child.

Neil shifted in his seat and stared at his cup without blinking. 'I don't even know the whole story; all I have are fragments. It was during the night and she seems to have woken from a nightmare. She was shouting in her sleep and he somehow thought it was against him and he became enraged. He beat her and beat her until the neighbours broke in because they heard her screaming. But it was too late. She'd lost so much blood and she died in hospital the following day.'

'Did you see her?' Somerled asked.

'I did,' Neil answered, and now looked up, nodding slowly.

'I did. Sometimes I seem to know – to be told – when things are going to happen. I never felt I knew Deirdre terribly well; I mean there were all manner of things I didn't know, that she hadn't told me. Yet there was a bond between us that went very deep. It didn't matter if I didn't see her for years, the moment we were together it was re-established, as strong as ever. Anyway, a few nights ago I had a particularly vivid dream. It was of someone taking an axe to a tree; a man was cutting down a tree with an axe and it was blood that ran from the trunk, not resin. I woke up and knew that whatever this was, whatever this meant, it had to do with Deirdre. And I went.'

Somerled nodded. He knew the dream, and the man in the dream. Was it really possible for two people to dream the same dream? And for a moment he thought of telling Neil all of it, all of this chapter he most likely knew nothing about. And then he wondered even now, with Deirdre dead, whether that would be right.

'I went up to Inverness by train, and I didn't think I was going to get there. The line was almost blocked by snow at the highest point; we must have been two hours late. I went straight to the house, still knowing nothing, heard a garbled account from the neighbours and went up to the hospital. There was no one else there. He's in custody, so that wasn't an issue. She came and went in sleep; she would see me and not know who I was. Sometimes she must have thought I was him; once she even asked if I was you. And then, all at once, she became completely lucid and she knew me. She seemed to realise there was very little time left and she asked me to open her bag. She said there was a picture there I had to take and give to you, that you would understand. She kept saying it, kept repeating it, as though she was frightened it wouldn't be done, might not happen. At first I thought it wasn't even there and then I found it.'

He held out a picture that fitted exactly in Somerled's palm. It was charred all round the edges. It was a black-and-white picture of a man standing in woodland. He was holding an axe and it was clear he had chosen a tree that had to be cut down. He was turning to the camera to smile. Not a whole, wide smile; it was almost as though it was reluctant, as though he had been disturbed and was taken aback. It was as if he was waiting for this to be over so he could get back to what he had come to do.

'Who is the man?' Neil asked.

Somerled looked up at him. He had been far away in his thoughts, so far away. He had never seen this picture before; he didn't even know exactly where or when it had been taken. But he knew enough.

'It's our father,' he said. 'It's somewhere in the woods near where we grew up.'

And he thought again of the last time he saw her, and thought now of how truly it had been the last time. And he thought of all the strangeness of time and of past things, how their childhood and growing up was deep within the rings of a tree. It existed and yet it had gone beyond reality. It was part of another world now.

'Well, that's what I had to give you,' Neil said, his eyes on the picture that Somerled still held in his palm.

'There will be no funeral, and I'm not sure just how many would have been there anyway. Her husband was fiercely jealous; he wanted her to have as few friends as possible, and I know that at least once when she and I talked she said that he knew nothing of our meeting. I'm sorry to be the bearer of such bad news, but I wanted to find you right away. I'm glad you were in the village today.'

He was already getting up to leave, pushing away as though eager to be gone. But Somerled caught his arm.

'How can I find you?' he said. 'I mean, if there's news, if there's anything . . .'

'Send a message through George: George knows where I am.'

And then he turned, as though relenting, and he looked at Somerled again, the dark eyes glittering.

'I believe that you and your wife are to have a child. Deirdre told me, in that bit of time when she was lucid. I wish you well. Here's to better times for us all, and may she be at peace at last.'

And then he was gone. Somerled had to sit down again, and Hugh suddenly spied him as he stood washing dishes. He started babbling about a car that had been half buried in a layby on the road to Inverness, how the woman inside had been lucky to escape with her life. And Somerled felt the way he once had when he was twelve years old; he had a fever one winter and for three days he was in his room at home. His mother was entertaining; she had rich guests from somewhere and their voices and laughter floated up from the sea room below. She had forgotten about him and he was thirsty. He sat upright, his back and head against thick pillows, and the room seemed to sway about him, it was like the cabin of a boat on an open sea. And all of him felt wrapped in cotton wool; there was a layer between him and the world.

He felt like that now, there in the gloom of the inn. This was the place where he had met Anna, but he was on his own now. The voice of Hugh was still there in his ear as he prattled on. But Somerled looked down at the picture in the palm of his hand and thought about all of it, about the many things that came together in that one image. Why had Deirdre wanted him to have it? Why had she wanted it to come back to him? Why should it be this picture from among them all, after everything their father had done to her? And why had it been burned, for the edges were charred and brittle. And he thought of how she herself had been burned by her husband, and he wondered if the two things were linked. There was so much he did not know; there was more in fact that he did not know than ever he would know.

The tea was grey and cold and he did not drink it. He paid for it all the same and listened to Hugh prattle about things that had disappeared and a new coat. He had stopped listening and he thanked him, went out into the winter and began the long walk home.

'Deirdre's dead,' he said when he came in, and he saw the oval of Anna's face as she looked up from the kitchen table. Everything was in slow motion as she dropped the knife and came over to him and held him and a dam broke inside him. He cried for Deirdre assuredly, but perhaps he cried also for this, for the stone wall that had come between him and Anna, which he did not properly understand and which he had never wanted to be there. He had not thought until then that it was possible to cry for two things. And he thought of it like two rivers; two different rivers that suddenly flowed together.

He put the photograph in the House of the Sparrow, to watch it and to wait somehow for the mystery of it to be revealed. He wanted to watch it on his own, to study every piece of it to know if there was something he was overlooking, something that Deirdre had intended him to find that he was forgetting. And other times he held it and thought simply that it was the picture of their shared story, neither more nor less. And the picture would never be complete; it would always be charred and brittle round the edges, with whole pieces missing. Their father was dead, Deirdre was dead, and their mother did not even know who she was. He was the only one that remained, and he well knew that his memories were broken and distorted and old. Yes, they were old; they had been half-buried all these years.

That Christmas they spent down at the house with Allan and Martha, the boys and Aunt Jessie. The men went down to the river to cut holly, and they were wet to the skin when they came back with two bags of the stuff. And Martha wheezed about the place; she did all the things she'd always done, just slower and with that struggle in her eyes. And Allan watched every step she took; he never once forgot her or neglected her, and Somerled saw it, kept seeing it.

And Aunt Jessie sat on the edge of it all like someone by a fireside who can still stretch their hands to its warmth and feel its glow on their face. She said almost nothing that whole Christmas and yet she was not forgotten; she was never neglected. And all Somerled wished was that Deirdre might have been there. He wished she might have known for once laughter and love without fear.

And Anna was sick with the child inside her that was growing every day. She was sick on Christmas morning and they walked together on a path she had loved as a child, and he remembered her words about how he didn't know her, and he resolved to learn more, to ask more.

He had had no proper time for fine carvings in the last weeks, so all the gifts he had planned to make were forgotten. Only one much older carving of a squirrel on a twig went to Aunt Jessie, and she was delighted with it, played with it like a child. But his gift for Anna was nothing; it was something she needed from the village, and he felt the inadequacy of it intensely. When they went back home it came to him what he could do; he'd begin work on things for the baby.

He set aside little fragments of time in the House of the Sparrow; he would go up there a few minutes early in the morning and come down to the house a little later than usual when she had called him. Anna never went in there, so he hardly needed to hide the things he was making. But he did so because he wanted to surprise her; he wanted to cheer her.

For once she had been the centre of attention at Christmas. How many weeks were there still to go and was she sleeping and eating properly? Did they still not know if it was to be a boy or a girl? She was shy of it all and yet he saw too that she was pleased; she was proud of all this meant and she was happy. Just sometimes as he sat there working in the half-light and straining his eyes, he remembered Jess and her words that night of the blizzard, and a shadow went through him. It was like a physical creature, and he felt its passing through his whole being. As he stopped carving, the tools still

112

in his hands, he would look out onto the late winter land and remember that night. All of it would rush back and he would wonder, what if she had been right? What if Allan was wrong after all? And he felt a tightness in his throat and the fear rose within him, and once he was on the point of dropping everything and going there and then to confess. For he had kept it from Anna, and most of the time it was gone, most of the time he believed it was for the best. And the shadow passed through him that day and he breathed again, began carving once more and told himself it was true – it was better that she did not know than that she did.

One day he had gone up to the House of the Sparrow and started work on a whole batch of ordinary things for the shop. He was working on the last of an eggcup, and he so little expected Anna's shout that he cut himself and swore softly. He got up and opened the door.

'Parcel for you,' she said, holding it out to him as though he could reach it from where he was. 'I thought it might be something exciting.'

He was down in a few steps, and he got blood onto the little packet. It was certainly heavy, whatever it was. They sat together at the kitchen table and she watched him as he tore the whole thing open and grumbled about the elaborateness of the packaging. In the end it was a little box of coins, with a card and a scribbled note on the back.

We will not require any more carvings for the time being.

He read the words over and over again, as though he did not understand the language in which they were written. Anna was talking to him; he knew she was saying things he could not hear and shaking his wrist.

'That's what I made for all those hundreds of hours of work! After they take away everything that's what I'm left with! There's no mortal point carving for a pittance like that. Do they take me for some kind of fool?'

He was shaking with rage and his eyes were red with grief. She said things to him but she knew herself it was useless, and she understood why. He wanted to go there and then and burn the whole pile of bogwood he had found at the lochs. What was the point of any of it? What was the point of carving more when this was all the reward?

But she stopped him in the end; she calmed him until he was empty, the anger sour in him but finished. They sat there together, silent, for a long time, until suddenly her eye caught sight of something beyond the door, fluttering this way and that in the breeze.

She held his arm and whispered. 'Look, Somerled! A snowdrop!'

He nodded, and his hand that still had its stain of dried blood crept out and sought hers. Together, though they had said nothing, they got up from the table and went to open the door and see it more clearly. They bent down to look at it.

'I can't bear to pick it,' she said, glancing round at him. 'All that struggle to fight through the frozen ground, only to be picked. At least not yet, and there'll be others.'

He looked at the ground, and then reached out to embrace her. 'Forgive me for all the ways I've failed,' he said. 'I've felt I've failed ever since I was a child, and I go on failing ... But I also go on getting up.'

She cupped his face in her hands and looked into his reddened eyes. 'And I believe in you, Somerled. I believe in what

114

you can do, and what you will do. And you have to teach this one to carve too!'

She patted her stomach and smiled and held him.

'I'd better do some work or there'll be nothing for the table when that baby's born!' He went back up the path, but now he worked instead on the surprises for Anna. He had no heart for eggcups and wooden spoons, not after the rejection of his real work that day. But while he worked he was thinking, racking his brains for a solution. For there had to be some better place for his carvings, somewhere that would value them and give him a good price. And he imagined how one day he might live from his work and that money alone, and he felt flooding his heart the warmth that the thought brought. And the sun bloomed through the glen and he looked up, blinded, and he knew that it was spring, that the winter was over at last. And he rejoiced, for everything might yet be all right.

There was no more word of Deirdre. He went into the post office now and again in the hope that George might call him over, that his face might light up as he saw him, telling him there was word from Neil, or that Neil himself was in the village. But George asked bright as ever for Anna as he sorted this and folded that behind the counter, that was all. And it was as though Deirdre had been swallowed by darkness. And he remembered the days in the west and sometimes could not fathom that she was dead. It seemed simply impossible.

That springtime they came up the glen, four men in grey uniforms. He heard them before he saw them; their laughter echoed down below on the track, and he got the scent of their tobacco too. He watched them, wondering where they were headed, and then realised they had turned and were making their way up the track. He tried to fathom what it might be they came for, and he scraped back his chair and went out to wait for them. A bird was singing; it was birdsong he didn't recognise.

'Well, and a good morning to you, Mr Stewart,' the first of them said, touching his cap. He was Aberdeenshire through and through.

Somerled said hello, waiting only for what might come next.

'We're here with a present for you. It's your father-in-law down in the village; he's paid for a phone line to come to your house. We're only up to tell you today, but we'll be back next week to start work.'

Anna came to the door, slow and careful, curious.

'I'm not sure,' Somerled frowned. 'I'll need to think about it.'

'What is it?' Anna asked, holding her hands under her belly. She shielded her eyes against the fierceness of the sun.

'Your father's given you the present of a telephone line, Mrs Stewart! He asked us to come up and tell you today!'

'Somerled, that's wonderful. We said only the other day we had to think of it! If anything were to happen with the baby . . .'

He turned and looked at her, thoughts swirling in his head. He blinked and his eyes searched, then at last he shrugged, looked away and rolled a stone with his foot. Reluctantly he nodded to them. 'All right then, all right. We'll see you back here next week.'

She touched his cheek when they had gone again. 'Why can't you take things that are given you? Why are you so proud? Isn't it a thing to be thankful for?'

He brushed away and past her, struggling with himself. 'Yes, but I want to give you these things too, not just have them given.'

And all that morning he thought of it and couldn't forget. He had almost begun another carving the other day, for he knew that a leaping salmon lay in the bogwood, and then the knife fell from his hand. What was the point? Where would he send it when he was done? No one wanted his work. No one. And he heard his father's words in his head, telling him he would never make anything in his life – nothing but a mess.

Yet he raged against the words too, and against the bleakness of his own heart. He fought for a way he believed had to be there.

He went to see Martha one day and she was out at the back of the house trying to hang up clothes. She had sat down on the wooden bench and was leaning forward, struggling to get her breath. He took a towel out of her hands, at first intending to hang it up, and then he saw the fear in her eyes and he simply put his arms around her and held her as she wept. What he said he didn't know. But Martha had been good to him and welcomed him; she had never said a word against him, and she was a fighter. She had the heart of a lion in that tiny frame of hers. And he felt the tears burn his own eyes. He cried as much for Allan as for her.

The men came and the telephone line was put into the house. New poles strode their way down to the village. Somerled asked if they would put up more, deeper into the glen. The men laughed as they drank the sweet tea from their flask;

what would be the point in that? There was nothing but rocks and ruins for twenty miles. And in the midst of his embarrassment, as he laughed, he thought again of the footprints in the snow and wondered whose they had been. And once more a strange darkness passed through him at the thought.

Anna telephoned her father to thank him for the present and Somerled had to speak too. It was a good enough idea and he was grateful; Anna had smoothed out the worst of his annoyance. But it was himself he raged at, for not being good enough, for failing. If only the labour of his own hands had earned this . . .

The spring flew past. Suddenly there were nests in the hedgerows and it was light before five in the morning. Anna grew afraid; sometimes she cried because she was afraid of what lay before her. He thought they did better, were gentler with each other. But there were days they stormed at each other too and everything seemed wrong. There were days it was hard to be in each other's company. Then sometimes he thought of Deirdre, of how lucky he was. And there had never been another word from Neil, though once or twice he had asked George, just in case.

There was a morning he was down in the village and he thought he would call on Allan. But only old Tom was there, sorting through piles of scrap metal. He turned round when Somerled came in, dour as ever.

'Allan's not here, he's back at the house. He's not worked here the last couple of days.'

That was it: not a word of explanation, not even a thought for Anna. Somerled had no wish to thank him and he didn't; he said no more and turned and went out. The sun came and the daffodils on the verges glowed like another thousand tiny suns. He was too warm; he had put on too many clothes and his back itched with heat.

When he went into the house he saw Allan there at the kitchen table. He stopped because he expected the older man to hear him and turn round. But he didn't. He sat there, turned away, all that great frame of his folded in on himself. He was more like a man in a painting than a living man, and all the words Somerled searched for faded. He turned away and went up the stairs on soft feet and looked into Martha's room. A butterfly was pattering against the glass; as the sun lit its wings he saw the red-brown markings that made its beauty.

'Martha?'

She opened her eyes and looked at him, drifted back from somewhere far away. She struggled to rise, and he frowned and shook his head, crouched down on the floor close to her.

'It's good to see you, Somerled,' she said, and her voice came from a dark place in her chest and was not hers, was not the old voice of light and laughter he remembered from the days when he first came here. Her hand searched for his and it was small and ice-cold. He would have replied to her but he didn't know where his own voice was; he didn't believe that he would find it. So he just held her eyes with his own; that was the most he could do.

'How is Anna?'

He nodded. He wanted to tell her she was still doing too much, still hanging up clothes and carrying wood and setting fires. But he just nodded.

'I hope your child will love the place where you live.'

A long silence; he knew she was gathering everything to say more.

'Do you know they believed that was a hill of fairies?'

She coughed, and that single cough became a violent fit of coughing that closed her eyes and doubled her up. She was so small; there was so little of her. And then, at last, there she was once more, breathing, and the eyes reaching out and finding.

'They used to leave out milk there,' she whispered, 'and they always believed it was taken.'

She closed her eyes and fought, fought. He nodded and nodded, even though it did not matter, for she could not see.

And he battled a grief he did not want her to see, and he knew suddenly that Allan was behind him. And he knew that he loved these two; he had never cared for the parents who had brought him up in their cold and loveless house. That was what they had been – nothing more than parents. But here he had known mother and father for the first time. And he saw too the love they had for the other; this bond that had held strong thirty years and more. They had grown together like two trees in a wood, and they had not grown apart. And he thought of this strong man now and what he would be when she was gone. How would he ever grow back after her going? How was it possible?

He left them together there and went back out into the light, and yet the sun seemed diminished and the daffodils' golden fire pointless. He went back up the track home, the bag heavy on his back, seeing nothing, and turning everything over in his head to find no answers. There was so much joy and so much pain; that was all that could be said in the end. That was all there was.

120

He cried more for Martha than ever Anna cried. And sometimes he found that strange and sometimes he forgot to think of it. Was it that she had enough to carry with all the weight of her child?

She was far away, as she was now when he came in to the house and put the bag down on the table and glanced at him. How well did he really know her, for all his trying? How far had he come?

But when the baby began at last, everything seemed to be as it should be. There was none of the snow that Anna had feared; the glen was in gold and not a whisper of wind. The doctor came as though he had been waiting for days, doing nothing, biding his time, and a nurse called Mairi Morrison, whose voice was like a song with the Gaelic that lay behind it. And everything began on the very day it was meant to, but Anna's eyes still met his – far away and frightened, as she pulled this way and that with pain. He said things that were useless and held on to the white hand that tore at his own. It was as though she was out on a great sea, and sometimes the waves took her and bucked her again and again and again.

Then there was calm and she looked at him and saw him. He put his hand through her soaking hair and for a second he saw her again, that first day she brought him into the inn.

And then the sea rose once more underneath her, and she cried out and fought this way and that. And he felt his love for her, but all he could do was hold her hand. And for a flash he thought of Allan too, how that was all he could do in the end for Martha, to hold her hand and tell her he loved her.

And when he looked again at the window he knew that it was growing dark, and he wondered how many hours had

121

gone. Anna was tired, tired beyond all reason. She cried and
the nurse's voice sang to her as she sat on the bedside. And
suddenly he was aware of the blood, of just how much blood
there was. He felt scared and babbled at the doctor, and the
man held his shoulder and all Somerled heard was the smile
in his voice. That and the fact that it wouldn't be long now;
she was almost there. And then all at once in the midst of the
blood and the smell and the mess, a small face. It cried like
a kitten and the wrinkles of its eyes squeezed tight against
the light. Somewhere he heard Anna's voice, and the voice
of Mairi Morrison, and suddenly he was holding this living
thing in the cradle of his arms, and he could not help but
weep. And he told Anna she had done well, that he loved
her, there in front of the doctor and the nurse in the sudden
strangeness of that place.

Then they were saying something else, and he never knew
afterwards all that they said. A whisper that was taken up and
repeated, and he listened, bewildered, scarcely able to believe.

'It's a boy.'

And perhaps it was Anna herself, for he was looking at her,
and she was smiling in the midst of it all, smiling in a way
that he understood, for he had been so sure it would be a girl.

So that meant it would be Finlay and one day Finn, for that
was what Anna had decided. She had woken up from a dream
one night in the darkness and told him; she had hugged him
and whispered it to him and he turned, mumbling still that he
knew it would be a girl.

And he saw the baby now in the fold of her arms below
him, how she kissed the matted hair of that head and looked
and kept looking with love. A shadow of fear passed through

him; it was just a flicker, just the blink of an eye, as he thought again what it meant, what it meant for the days to come.

He found himself making tea, and there was shortbread in the cupboard. He offered the doctor a dram of whisky and the doctor clapped his shoulder again and said that if he'd had a dram for every baby he'd seen coming into the world he would have been under the daisies a long time ago. And Anna slept, the baby still in her arms, as they sat in the cold of the kitchen at four in the morning, drinking scalding tea and eating shortbread. And he had no idea what to talk about; he could think of nothing to say and he looked at both of them and smiled, and all of them laughed together. And he thought of the strangeness and the wonder of the world, and asked himself if perhaps for a moment they did too.

And then the doctor and Mairi left. Somerled watched the car's tail-lights until they were nothing more than ghostly glows. He was about to pad into their room when he remembered something. He dragged on his boots and went outside into the raw silence of the dark, and up the path to the House of the Sparrow. He brought out the cradle he had made, and the little chair that one day would be the right size for the boy Finn, and back he went to the house. Just before he turned inside, he felt something behind him. He swung round, soundlessly, and there on the post beyond the house wall was an owl. It was impossibly white in the shadows, and the yellow globes of its eyes held him. He turned away a second, thinking of something, and when he looked back it lifted away on cloth wings.

He put the cradle and the little chair where Anna would see them when she woke, undressed and lay down beside them. The room was filled with a pearl light; it was nearing five in the morning and the shadow was vanishing a little every minute. He did not think that he would sleep and yet he did. He slept almost there and then, but it was a shallow place, almost not there at all. He might have slept for ten minutes or two hours; when he did waken it was because of a sound, a sound that went on and on and on and would not stop. He opened his eyes and listened, but still he couldn't understand what it was. Then he moved and lifted his head and it was the ringing of a telephone. He got up, naked, and went through the house towards it. He picked up the receiver and softly asked who was there.

'It's Allan. Martha died at dawn this morning.'

'And Finlay was born about the very same time.'

Still Anna slept on, that tight bundle held in her arms. He watched them for a while when he came back into the room. He didn't waken her, not then, for the day had hardly begun and he had seen her exhaustion. He did everything he could: he lit the fire, he made a pan of broth, he cut bread. The house smelled of wood smoke and warm bread. He sat at the kitchen table and wished he could have told Deirdre. He did not cry when he thought of her, just sat there and thought of all he had known of her and all he had never known.

Anna was not able to go to her own mother's funeral. She still had no strength and the nurse came and stayed with her for the time that Somerled was away. The whole village closed; the teachers came from the primary school, and with them many of the older children. But it was the coming of the old men that Somerled marvelled at. Men who had worked with horses, who had worked on the land and had the land in their hands; they came from old cottages and places hidden under the hills, as though some inaudible bell had summoned them. For all of them had known the man with the great hands, and they had loved him, and they came now to honour the memory of the woman he had loved all his life. One shepherd walked ten miles to the village to be there that morning, over fields bright and vivid green under the sunlight.

The minister, John Grant, had been at Martha's bedside time after time that last year. He had come to talk to her, to talk to her when all she could do was listen because even a single spoken word was sufficient to bring back the cough that took away all her breath. He brought her good stories of his own, growing up in the Highlands, stories that made her forget her fear of the shadow that grew with every passing day. And sometimes he sat at the kitchen table with that big, strong man her husband, whose shoulders quivered because he could not bear what lay ahead. And he wept too.

Allan wept now, on that beautiful blue day when the whole glen came to remember her. But he said they should not cry just the same, for it was over and she had gone to rest and there was no more pain for her to face. But Somerled cried, for he remembered the bright Martha busy in the kitchen, a bumblebee that never stopped darting here and there, full of what she had to do. And Somerled thought that he never remembered her saying an ill word of anyone.

He thought of Allan now, as he stood at the window that same night. His two sons were with him and he feared they would drink into the morning. They would drink until they laughed again, and the dawn would bring only the memory of their loss. For it would be a Martha-less sky and a Martha-less light, and he wondered as he had wondered a thousand times before how that great man would ever carry the weight of it on his shoulders. For he had loved with all his heart, and Somerled knew that he would not love again.

Finn fretted in his sleep; a thin, milky crying, and Anna drew him tighter in to her breast without waking. Somerled wasn't tired and his fingers twitched with the desire to carve. He slipped up the path to the House of the Sparrow and crouched on the floor to sift through that strange gathering of bogwood. They were like bones, he thought; the bones of ancient things that had given themselves up from the dark peat floors of the lochs. And he remembered the axe he had found on the shore of the island, and saw in his mind's eye the man who had made it. He found a piece of wood that might have a badger inside it, and he knew he would find it for Allan. Martha had loved badgers, no matter how often the keepers told her they were vicious beasts and carried tuberculosis. She would smile and shake her head.

'I can never help loving their bonnie wee faces!'

He took the wood and his tools down to the house so he could keep an eye on Anna and Finn, so he could be there if she was suddenly awake and wanting something. He crouched at the unlit grate, and pieces of dark wood flicked one by one from the knife. Outside it refused to get dark; the sky grew only a deeper and deeper blue, and he heard the whirring songs of the woodcock about the house and the soft lift and fall of the wind. And he carved until his eyes could see no longer and the dark had fallen at last. And when he looked up he met Anna's eyes and knew she had been watching him. And he smiled shyly, like a boy, and she smiled softly as she lay there on her side. He had all but found the badger.

When the summer came in earnest the days stretched out, strange and endless. The river seemed like a starved creature, its bones standing out and no strength left in its flow. Its pools lay dusty and thin.

There was a day he went up to his loch, the loch that lay like a long eye in the heather, and he found the island was an island no longer. There was a peat shore two feet wide the whole way round, and that shore was broken by deep crevices and cuts. He felt an eeriness about the place and could not bring himself to go out to the island. He stood looking, appalled and almost frightened, and he had no wish to stay. He had hoped he might climb to find the wind but there was nothing. The day hung dead blue, and dry things crackled beneath his feet.

He could not carve. He felt there was nothing in his hands. He turned the pieces of bogwood and could not see what lay inside them. They were bones, nothing more than ancient memories of wood. He had heard nothing from the shop in Inverness, not a word, and now his pride would not let him ask if they might take more. He looked at the scattering of fragments and felt he had failed utterly; there was no more he could do and he had lost his sight. He wanted to tell Anna and yet he did not; he bit his lip and the blood came, sore in the dry cracks of skin.

He had taken the badger to Allan. It was a few weeks after Martha's passing and he found him there in the kitchen, looking out of the window the same way he had done when she was so ill upstairs, and he almost could not bear to see her. Aunt Jessie sat outside in the sun; as long as she could knit she was content. She wore the same thick woollen things summer and winter. She lived deep in her own world, all but deaf, content with memories.

Somerled put the badger on the table. It tapped the wood as he set it down and Allan turned round. Once upon a time his face would have broken into smiling and he would have held out his hand. Now his eyes were far away and did not seem to come back. He looked away, to that invisible place he stared at. He did not even think to ask for Finn, though he had held the boy, and the embers of pride were there. He did not say anything at all for a long time.

'I want to go away and I don't know how to get there. All this struggle and for what? I used to have no time and now I have no end of it. I don't know what to do, Somerled.'

And when he said that he turned to him, and the great hot grief was bright in his eyes, and Somerled had no words for him, nothing that might have assuaged his sadness or tried to push it away. He wanted to tell him he had been more of a father to him than the man who had brought him up all those years ago in the west, but he did not know what the words were. He could only hold his gaze and nod, for he understood. He knew that he spoke the truth.

The following day it was Anna that went to be with him, and she did not take Finn with her. She carried things for the house, for now that her mother had gone its corners were filled with shadow and it had slipped into its own dust. For the first time she left Finn with his father; there was a whole list of things he had to do and another whole list of things he had not to do. Then she was gone, out into the same blue cloudless day, and even the sound of her feet on the stones had faded. Finn lay on the table, wide awake, his head rolling round to look at his father, and the dark eyes were like sloes, and their intensity almost frightened him. The boy watched his father, his eyes searching upwards all the time.

And Somerled thought how sure he had been this child would be a girl, and the days and the years galloped ahead in his mind and he wondered how it would be then. What did he have to give to this child of his? What inheritance was there? He would teach him to carve, yet what if that was the last thing his child wanted? What if this place and all it held was nothing but a torment to him, if he wanted away instead to the noise and thrill of the city? Would he accept it? Was he ready for all that he could try to give him to be flung back in his face? He grasped the tiny hand that was so small in his own, and he whispered things of comfort. Yet was it to comfort the child or to comfort himself? Would he fail as much as his own father had failed with him? The fear rose inside him so that for a moment he felt he could not breathe. What sort of a father could he be when he had known no love in the house of his parents? Would it not have been better to tell Anna everything, to tell her there was a chance the poison would pour from one generation to the next?

He did all he had been told to do and waited for her to return at eight in the evening. He was watching for her out of the window, and she had told him that by then Finn would be asleep. Finn was nothing of the sort; he lay watching his father, his dark eyes moving all the time, half-interested in the toys he was given – the sparkling things he held in his tiny hands. The glen was filled with lemon light and there were birds flying. He wished that Anna would return so he could go out into it. There was that feeling he sometimes had that he had to go out into the light there and then, because soon it would be passed and gone, that the day would be lost for ever.

Half past eight came and there was still no sign of Anna. He could have telephoned to find out what was happening, but it would have meant disturbing Finn and he wanted the little soul to sleep. There was a last half bottle of milk that Anna had made up for him; the tiny paws of hands clutched the glass, the dark eyes looked at Somerled, searching and searching.

He wondered what his parents would have said of their grandson. The endless cycle of parties and the boats and their quest for status would have faded by now; perhaps they would have had time to love him. And would that in turn have brought back the memories of all he had not had? He simply did not miss them. He did not think of them. It was a story in a book whose pages had been written a long time ago. He had shut the book and knew where it was on the shelves, but he neither missed it nor needed it. One day he would take Finn to the west; he would show him all the places he had found and treasured, but he would not go back to the house. The only thing that lay buried there was sadness, his own and Deirdre's.

'Once upon a time there was a boat,' he whispered, and Finn's eyes watched him as before, the milk all but guzzled. The words had come without thinking, and yet now they were out they were the start of a story. He glanced out of the window and still there was no sign of Anna.

'A man lived by the sea and went out every day with his boat. It was a beautiful place, with white sandy shores and blue-green water. And one day when he was out in the boat it was deathly calm. He found himself looking down into the water and he saw that it wasn't just bottomless dark but that there were palaces there. They looked as if they were carved out of pure gold, and he knew that never in his life had he seen so much beauty before. He wanted to be there, because he knew that his life out of water was lonely and empty, but he had no idea how he could get there. And all he could do every day was to dream of a world that he couldn't reach.'

He had no idea if the story was finished or what on earth it meant or where it had come from. He almost felt shy of having spoken it aloud in front of Finn; he felt foolish. He looked round yet again to see if Anna was coming and she wasn't.

'Where is that mother of yours?' he whispered, holding both of Finn's hands tight in his own and leaning in close to him. 'What is she doing and where has she gone?'

And all at once he thought about what it would be like if it were to happen. If he were simply to come back and find her gone, both she and Finn. A hollowness opened deep inside him. Yet what did he give her? Had he really made the place he once dreamed of making so special? Or was that the truth, that every place, whatever dreams lay behind it, became in the end the same as anywhere else? Was it true that you failed to see perfection when it lay all around?

In the end Finn fell asleep just the same, but it was a strange sleep that almost unnerved him. He didn't even properly see the moment Finn drifted away. His eyes were still open, glassy and dark, and he seemed almost not to breathe at all. There was a fleck of milk on his bottom lip.

And suddenly Anna was behind him; he hadn't heard her and he got a fright and was annoyed both with himself and with her.

'Couldn't you have telephoned?' he blazed in a half-whisper. 'I was worried sick and it's half past nine! You said you'd be back by eight!'

'And my father was miserable, partly because of the badger you gave him. You never told me you were taking it and he was upset with it. I stayed there to comfort him! Would you have had me leave him in misery?'

'I made the badger for him because I knew how special they had been to your mother! I was only trying to do something good!'

She looked away from him, standing there saying no more, watching over Finn. He lay just as he had done before, on his back, with his head turned a little to one side. Even from there, Somerled caught the shining of his half-open eyes. He remembered all he had thought as he had watched him. He went closer, awkwardly, searching for the right words.

'He took a long time to go to sleep. I tried to do everything.'

'Do you know that I still haven't seen him smile?' Her voice was louder than his. She didn't look at him yet, but only at Finn.

'Isn't he still too young? Isn't it that?' He pushed back a darkness inside him that made his heart pound.

'But it's more than that. It's more than that he doesn't smile. He sometimes seems to have a sadness in him, almost like a shadow.'

And then the fear came over him like a cloak. He went over and clutched her shoulders, pulled her round to look at him. He felt dizzy with fear but he knew that now she had to know. And he poured out the whole story, of the night of the blizzard and how the travellers had been there. Of his anger and how he had sent them on their way, and the words that Jess had thrown at him before they went. He told her every single detail; he brought her back to that day and set it all in front of her. And he prayed she might laugh at him, tell him it was nothing, that the words of a traveller meant less than nothing. And she stared at him, until the words had run out and there was no more to be said. And even then she was silent and still watched him, and he breathed and in the silence he heard the tiny, quick breathing that was Finn's. And he waited, wanting her to speak, to be anything but silent.

'Then you can go and find them. You can go and find them and beg them on your knees to take anything away they left here. My father may have laughed at it, but I won't. There was a boy at school who died because of the travellers. He mocked one of them and they put a curse on him. He drowned. He drowned about six weeks later and all of us remembered. So you damn well find them, however long it takes. And you're not welcome in this house before you do.'

It was her cold he feared then; the shadow he saw in her. He knew there was nothing he could do to bring her close to him. That was what chilled him. His mouth was dry; he watched her a few seconds, as though somehow daring to believe she might relent, and she only turned away to bend over Finn, to wrap him more tightly in warmth. And he turned, still dizzy, and blundered away, and she did not even look up.

133

He did not think about what he should take and so he took nothing. He stumbled from the house as though he had been pushed. He had never heard a greater silence. The sky ahead of him into the west still held a pale orange glow; above and around him there was only white-blue and not a single cloud. He found himself heading down from the house to the main track, not thinking properly, in a kind of stupor. So many things circled his mind: Anna, the baby, the travellers, Allan, the carving. He looked back once towards the house but the windows were dark. He stood a moment, as though somehow she might see him at the same time and call to him to come back. But there was nothing, and he could only turn away.

And where was he to go? He had no mortal idea where he would find the three who had come with their horses, on their way west through the glen.

He found himself going up the glen rather than down, but it wasn't that he thought about his direction. He was following nothing; there was no plan in his mind. He had nowhere to begin and nothing to find in the village. He simply stumbled away from a house to which he could not return. That night of snow flickered through his mind; he saw the lathering flakes in front of his face in the orange-blue of the summer night. And he heard the words that were spoken to him, and saw himself fallen backwards into the snow, as the three began west with their horses. Why had he not called them back? Why had he not opened his mouth? They could have stayed the night in the House of the Sparrow and none of this would have happened. Because even if the curse had not been real, it had become real now: a self-fulfilling prophecy that had broken him away from Anna, perhaps for ever.

134

He came clattering down over the rocks to the river that was no river at all. There was almost no sound to it; the water was held in glass pools by the bones of the rocks. He stared round, his mouth half-open, and for a second he thought that all this was the curse, all of it was linked. Perhaps it might never rain again.

But there was still a part that ran, over towards the far side. He caught the flicker of the water as it danced, and he scrabbled over the loose stones, his ankles buried now and then in lukewarm liquid. He squatted and cupped the blue water in his fingers. Again and again he lifted his dripping hands, but it did not satisfy. It filled him, but it did not satisfy. And he thought again of the curse, as though all the world had somehow been darkened by his foolishness and by the words of the three travellers who had been denied shelter one winter night.

And then it was he turned and looked upstream. Perhaps he heard a murmur, but afterwards he could remember nothing. The river stretched up the glen almost straight at that point, and far away he saw a thin blue pencil of smoke rising from the river stones, and he caught movement. He got up and his feet squeaked in the stones. There was someone there; there must be, or else it was the last smoke of a fire that had been lit earlier that day. He went back to the side of the river he had left and began walking up the glen once more; not fast, just steady. His feet might have been the only sound in the world as they swished through the long grass. The alders and birches that hung over the river were carved out of shadows; the river was only a breath, a soft exhalation as it drifted eastwards. He walked and walked and walked.

135

'. . . and I said to Josie that she'd damn well better give me the money before Frank got wind of it. Can you imagine what he'd do if he found out? You know Frank, he's hardly one to ask questions first and keep his fists in his pockets. And fortunately Josie saw sense . . .'

He heard them before he saw them; he heard the words and understood them and they meant nothing at all. And he listened to them intently as his feet went soft through the grass, as though if he concentrated enough they would suddenly become clear.

And then they stopped; right in the middle of the story they stopped, and as he kept walking he saw the two figures hunched on the shore, their white faces turned to watch him, and it was the remains of their fire that lay beyond them, the wood fallen into black ash.

'And what the hell are you wanting?'

It was the same voice that had spoken that asked the question. He smelled the sweetness of cigarette smoke, and he heard it in the voice. He went down over the last yards of the bank and his feet were in the shingle, the shingle that normally was deep under water. There was a blackened kettle between them, a bottle of whisky, a mouth organ. He went so far and no further, crouched down on his knees on the hard stones and there was no smile, only the hard eyes of the one who had spoken, following him all the time, watching him.

'I'm looking for someone called Jess,' he said, and his own voice felt strange and hardly his own.

But the same man began looking all round him, lifted the jacket he was sitting on and peered at the ground.

'Jess? Jess? I don't see a Jess here. No, definitely no one of that name here. You see anyone called Jess, Tam? Nah, didn't think so.'

And he sat down and stared at Somerled once more. He fished a packet of cigarettes out of his pocket, took one and lit it. But he did everything in a hard and exaggerated way, and when he'd finished he looked again at Somerled, his eyes the same.

'I'm trying to find three travellers who passed our house on the way up the glen last winter. Two men and a woman. All I know is that the woman was called Jess. They had horses with them.'

His voice was his own now. He had no more to lose. And they didn't interrupt. The one called Tam was frowning, looking over at the other.

'Would that not have been Jess Stewart, her that was married at one time to Alec Tyler? I'm sure she's been down here in the past, though where the hell they would have been going's anyone's guess . . .'

And the voices muttered together, trying to work it out. They spoke over each other sometimes, offering ideas and changing their minds. And all at once as he stared at the shore between the two of them he saw something else; a small tin box that was half full of round white things. And for a moment he couldn't think what they were, and then he realised that they were pearls. These folk were pearlfishers; they had come to the Lyon to fish for pearls. But maybe they had no licence and knew it; maybe that was why they had been so suspicious when he came down out of nowhere to speak to them.

'It would have been Jess Tyler,' said the first, a new cigarette between his lips. 'And she's either in Dundee or up in Sutherland. And why should you want to find her anyway?'

And so he told them, more or less the same words he had spoken to Anna that same evening. He didn't look at them but they looked at him, and he smelled the sweetness of their cigarettes. And the only other sound was the river as it meandered east, stone by stone.

'And why did you wait until now?' the first man asked when Somerled was done.

Somerled lifted his face to look at him. 'Because I think she might be right. I think there is a shadow.'

The first man reached for the bottle that lay half-buried in the shingle. He fished out three mugs from a bag; old, white chipped things, and he splashed some yellow into each of them. He held out one for Tam and one for Somerled. It was the last thing in the world Somerled wanted, but he wasn't about to refuse. He raised his mug to them.

'So you reckon Jess cursed your bairn? Because you didn't let them stay?'

He heard the mockery in the man's voice; he saw the glint in his eyes as he glanced at Tam. And suddenly he wanted away; there wasn't a thing they could give him. And they were travellers too.

'We don't go round cursing folk. That's just another myth to demonise us. We may have a clearer sight of the future, but that's another matter. And both of us know Jess Tyler well enough. She was likely to be teasing you. But she may have seen a shadow that was there all the same. Maybe it's the stones that have done it. You should go up and speak to Bob Bell! Would you not say, Tam?'

He saw the wink. He swallowed the last of the yellow fire. 'What stones? And who's Bob Bell?'

The first man smiled now; Somerled saw the gold flash in his teeth.

'You live so long in a glen and you don't know that! Bob Bell lives up at the loch, however many miles further on. He's the keeper of the stones. They're as old as the hills, if not older! He takes them out on the first of May; brings them back at the end of October. They're the guardians of the glen. You don't cross the stones or you'll bring bad luck. So maybe that's what you did! It's more likely than that Jess Tyler put a curse on you, that's for sure!'

They were laughing at him and he got up from the shingle. 'Well, thanks for the whisky. I'll go and try and find him. And good fishing to you.'

'There's no good fishing because there's no damn water in the river!'

They didn't say goodbye; they took up the low murmur of their talk, the same sound he had heard as he walked up the riverbank towards them. And he went on along the bank, following the river that was no river at all, and he thought of the time when he came here first – walking out of the west, nothing but his father's axe with him and all the anger he had carried so long. He had seen nothing; he had just battled on blind, and he had drunk from the river. That was all he had noticed.

And then he thought of the only other time he had come this way, heading up the glen, to find the gold for Anna's ring. And he thought of it now and it seemed strange to him and hard to believe. He had been desperate to find that gold for her, and what was it worth now? It was just another ring, and its story all but forgotten.

And he followed the riverbed and all that was left of its water on and on and on. It seemed to take such a long time to reach the waterfall and the rocks, and it was as changed as the ring he had brought from its gold. He could scarcely believe it was the same place. A white flutter sought its way between the boulders. The pools remained; black pools of water that were ringed with green, a brilliant green film that was soft to the touch. He plunged his hand and arm into one of the pools and the water was warm, eerily warm.

He had to climb over that rubble of rocks to reach the other side. There was still sufficient light; the day hung blue and perfect, and a full moon made of cobwebs rose over the hills at his back. He fell once, for the rocks were slippery with slime, and he saw when he looked later that the base of his hand was thick and sticky with blood. But then he came to the river and stood there, and as his heart thudded in his chest, he looked over at a cottage and at a loch that lay beyond. And as he looked and looked and regained his breath he felt that somehow he stood on an edge of the world. Yes, this was an edge of the world – those were the words that came to him as he stood there. And he remembered the day he had looked down on this place, wondering, from the loch he visited on the hill behind the house. But he had never noticed the house before.

Now it was beautiful; all of it lay like a painting, and the sky in the west not a pure blue, but a melding of blue and white and yellow. And from somewhere he heard the coal rasp of a raven, and he remembered the pair of them, but he could see nothing at all.

There was a light in the cottage and he started over the stony ground, making straight for it. And he thought then that his mouth was sour with whisky; he spat and it made no difference, and he thought too that he had brought no gift, and he wondered why he should even think such a thing. Yet that would have seemed right, to have brought a gift. And as he reached out to knock on the wooden frame of the door, it opened before him and he all but fell inside.

'Well, Somerled Stewart, what brings you here?'

There was a fire even though there was no need of one, and he saw fiddles around the walls. The small man in front of him sank back in his chair and his bald head shone. He set to packing the bowl of a pipe full of tobacco, and it was as though he had forgotten the question he had asked. But it was as though perhaps his question had been more of a statement, as if he knew the answer without having to wait for it.

And Somerled stood there, in the heat of that tiny room, and a deerhound stretched up from somewhere in the shadows and came and searched his right hand for food. It was the hand that had been hurt on the rocks and he saw it wet with the dog's mouth. The half-dried blood was wet and shining.

'You know me and I don't know you.'

The man just laughed as he lit his pipe. But Somerled knew well enough that this must be Bob Bell, and he knew too that it was Bell's footsteps he had seen in the snow, the prints that had somehow unnerved him. He sat down, even though he had not been asked to sit, and the dog followed him.

The other snapped his fingers, and the dog padded over

and lay in front of him. The head went down between the thin, grey paws and the eyes watched Somerled, unblinking.

'I know you, and I know all about you.'

The air filled with pipe smoke and all at once Somerled felt sleepy. He could have fallen asleep in the glow of that orange hearth. He fought sleep and he looked at the eyes of the man and they seemed to dance; they shone and danced.

'I never knew about the stones,' he found himself saying as he shifted to sit up higher. 'I heard about the stones tonight, from the pearlfishers. I had never heard of them before.'

Bob Bell leaned forward, and Somerled saw that his eyes had changed. They had darkened, as though he had said something wrong, something foolish. He had talked nonsense; what had made him utter a word about the stones? All that might have been the foolery of the travellers and nothing more . . .

'I live here, and I make shoes and fiddles. I have as little to do with the village as I can. This is the watershed of Scotland. That river you followed is the first one that flows east. Beyond my house is the first burn that flows west. This is a special place. This is an ancient place. Maybe there was someone living here in the Bronze Age. And they were carrying out the stones then, spring and autumn. And I'll do it until I die, and God knows what'll happen after that. So why did you come here?'

Somerled babbled. Out of his sour, dry mouth came misshapen words and thoughts. He talked about Anna and Finn, about last winter, about the travellers. He talked about all he had tried to do. About all he had wanted to find and make. And he started to cry; like a fool he began crying, hunched forward where he was and Bob Bell looking at him, his eyes like gorse petals, his mouth half-smiling.

'Well, you can ask the stones. You can stay up there and ask them, but God knows if they'll give you an answer.'

'Is it possible to upset the stones? To offend them?'

Bob Bell looked at him. 'They're stones, Somerled. They've been carried out to their patch of ground maybe five thousand years, and they've had children. That's the truth; that's what the old folk in the glen will tell you. The two big stones are the Cailleach and the Bodach, the Old Woman and the Old Man. She's the important one; she's the one that counts. Offend her and you're in trouble. And over the centuries other stones have been added, other river stones from the Lyon. They're queer things, with strange heads. And instead of talking to you about them let me take you to meet them. Stay there and ask your questions. You can sleep by the burn and see what comes to you.'

The dog, who seemed to have no name, came with them. The man put no guard on the fire; he only took a stick that stood against the wall and went out into the blue silence of the night. They didn't walk together; the man led and he followed. It was hard to keep up with him; his shadow seemed to move effortlessly among the boulders, as Somerled stumbled at his back. He could barely see his own feet; he could only make out the vague black silhouettes of the ridges, and the still glass of the loch. They went round the northern edge of the water and up a tiny glen. A stream chinked through the middle of it; Somerled could just make it out.

'There they are. And don't touch them.'

Bob Bell had crouched down in the near-darkness and

Somerled joined him. At first he saw nothing at all, and then he saw them growing out of the darkness. Stones that were set upright, with what might have been small heads and bottle-shaped bodies. A breath of wind came, and he heard it in the grasses and the rocks. And it came to him that it was as lonely now as ever it had been.

'Why did they set them out here to begin with?'

'They believed in the goddess. There's folk think the name Lyon is much older than Gaelic, that it goes right back to those Bronze Age farmers. They wanted good, safe harvests and so the Cailleach and the Bodach were put out every year; they were looked after so bad things wouldn't happen. They have power all right. If you believe.'

Somerled looked and saw his smile in the blackness, and it was uncanny. He stayed there, looking at Somerled and not moving, with just that smile. And the wind came again from the west, stronger than before, and Somerled stood up because it would blow him over.

'And do the travellers have any links with the stones?'

Bob Bell stood up himself. 'This has been an ancient road across Scotland, from west to east. Old as the hills. And it was the travellers' road. So yes, they'd leave a gift for the Cailleach whenever they'd pass. They wouldn't leave Glen Lyon without giving a gift.'

And Somerled thought again of that night and of the words that Jess had spoken, and he wondered. He wanted to ask more but he didn't know how, and he feared the answers he might be given. The dog sought his hand in the darkness, the same hand and its blood.

'Well, I'll leave you here and you can see what comes to

you! Look for me in the morning if you want; I'm up at dawn every day. And I hope you find what you're wanting to find!'

He had no desire to go back with the man, but he had still less desire to sleep the night there. He looked and saw the last shadow of the dog before it and its master vanished. And the breeze came once more. He looked up at the sky and knew he should be unafraid, that he should rejoice in the blue emptiness of the heavens and their fields of stars. Yet he felt the ancient story of this place; he remembered that this was the watershed, he remembered that this was the way the travellers came when they crossed Scotland. And a sudden thought struck him; what if they should come back now and cross his path? It was beyond madness, and yet the fear of it gripped him nonetheless. The travellers knew these ancient stones, and perhaps they were able to take their power for themselves, for good or ill. And he crouched there and was afraid, and even then he wondered if he was afraid because of the stories he had heard, or because there really was something to fear in that place.

And all at once he began thinking about Anna and Finn. He was barred from his own house by his own stupidity, and he knew in his heart he could not blame Anna for her judgement. He suffered now for his selfish folly the previous winter, and he thought again how he might find Jess. He imagined himself talking to her in the inn, leaning over one of the tables, imploring her to take away the shadow she had left in his boy. And he saw her face as he imagined it, and her nodding, and her taking his hand and promising all would be well. All would be well when he went home. And he scraped back his chair and got up, and thanked her, and he began running and running up the glen ...

Something moved close to him and he started, turned in the direction of the noise and watched, listened. He remembered nights like this on the west coast in childhood, and he realised he felt no different. Perhaps in darkness we are always the same, he thought. And he wished he had some kind of light with him, or matches for a fire – something that might keep out the utter blackness. But he had brought nothing; he had left the house with empty hands.

This was a dead place, he thought. He was not even certain why the words came to him, but he considered them. Was it possible there were dead places, places so wild and remote they were barren? Here the only thing was the wind; wind and water. It came to him that even if he wanted to follow the path back to Bob Bell's place it would be impossible; he'd risk breaking his neck on the rocks. He would have to stay here until dawn, and the knowledge of that crept up his back and neck like a cold hand.

He looked back, and he saw that the stones were clear to him now. His eyes had grown accustomed to the dark and they stood there in their cluster; the two parent stones and their children. And it flashed across his mind that this was no more than pagan nonsense; how could some stones have governance over a glen? And then he wondered if it had always been that way in the beginning, back in the Bronze Age, that every glen had such stones and such offerings. This was the last place, the last of the lot of them.

And he thought about things that had gone wrong in the last year and more. He thought of Martha's death and he thought of Deirdre's, and he wondered if it was of his doing that she had died as she had. He wondered if the very distance between him and Anna was his fault, and that all of it was in the shadow of the stones.

He curled into himself on the ground and wondered how he ever would sleep. Yet he drifted into a strange place all the same; he was carving a piece of wood and it was of an unknown figure. He saw his hands working at its shaping but he had no idea what it was he carved. He knew he was in the House of the Sparrow; he felt himself there, and then the same noise came at his back and he turned round, terrified, his heart thudding in his chest.

Why had he not said to Bob Bell there was neither point nor need to spending the night here? He wondered at his own folly, and that brought him back to the travellers and the shadow. What would he do to have it taken from Finn? Where was he to begin? Was it really here he should start? Could it be that this huddle of river stones held all the power of the glen? Had they once brought him here, when he crossed Scotland with his axe and settled here?

He slipped in and out of dreams; afterwards he could not tell what had been real and what imagined. He felt a figure watching over him from the hill behind, and yet how was it possible to see anything against this darkness? He heard the voices and laughter of children at the burn, but he did not catch the actual words they spoke.

And then he knew that he was dreaming. A tall figure was coming towards him over an open field, and it was a pure, blue day. The light was perfect and he stood watching the figure for what seemed an eternity, but the person was always too far away to see their face. And then at last they stood in front of him and he realised it was Finn, Finn as he would become. And he held in his right hand the axe that Somerled had brought with him from the west. He looked at his father and then he bent and began digging the ground below him with his bare hands. The earth was soft and crumbled, and it was not long before he had made a kind of grave. He laid the axe inside, softly as though it was made of skin, and he covered it so the earth and the field looked undisturbed. Then he got up once more, and the dark and beautiful eyes looked right at his father.

'The shadow is in you, not me,' he said, and a second longer he remained there, staring, before he turned round and walked away once more. And Somerled wanted to run after him; he remembered the father of the Prodigal Son and he wanted to run with all his strength and bring him back. But he did not know if he could; his feet remained just where he stood beside the buried axe.

A long time later he awoke and his mouth was full of grass; his face had slipped into the wet ground. He knew that he had slept, but it was impossible to be sure if it had been for half an hour or four hours. It was still as dark as ever and he curled deeper into himself with the cold. And then he did sleep, full and deep, and he passed beyond a land of dreams into nowhere, into a good and safe place that could not haunt him. When next he was aware of anything, a curlew mourned miles above him in the thin blue skies of earliest morning. He opened his eyes like a newborn and came back slow and strange from that distant land. And he guessed it was four in the morning, and he staggered up and over to the stream; he cupped his hands and drank and drank, and the taste at last of the travellers' whisky was washed from his mouth.

He went back and crouched beside the stones and they were smaller than he had imagined them. But all his sense of fear had passed; what did he think these stones could really do to him and his son? He still did not dare touch them, but he bent his face close to them and looked at every side and shadow of them. They were river stones, worn by the long centuries – two much larger and four much smaller. They were stones and nothing more.

He got up and knew that he was hungry. He remembered Bob Bell's words, but he had no wish to go back to his cottage this morning. He tried to follow a different way, but it was impossible. The glen was a bottleneck, and to do other than walk out of the glen's throat would mean clambering about high on rocky escarpments. The fastest and easiest way back was the one they had taken the evening before.

He waited for Bob Bell's call of angry surprise as he hurried past, not thirty yards from the fellow's doorway, but there was nothing. The day was already warm; the skies clear as they had been for six long weeks.

He realised that he was walking home, that he had nowhere else to go. He imagined the things he might say, and all of them seemed foolish and useless in the end. All he could say was that he was sorry, and he did not know any more if that would be enough. And he thought of what he had built with his own hands, and of what he had sought to build with his hands, and he wondered if any of it remained.

He came to the place where the pearlfishers had been and there was no sign of their presence but for one mussel shell.

It was like an ear, the inside of it lined with mother of pearl. But it was empty; no pearl lay inside, not even the tiniest grain or seed. He threw it towards the thin water of the river and it caught the light before it fell among the rocks and broke. He stood there a moment longer; he realised that he was frightened to go home. She had told him not to come back until the shadow was lifted and he had done nothing; in effect he had given up.

But he had to go all the same. He went softly up the hill track and he rounded the corner to go towards the door, his heart hammering, and there he met the minister, John Grant.

'I was taking off my boots before bringing in half the dust from the glen!' Then he stopped and looked at Somerled again. 'You're tired, man – your face is full of tiredness. I'm sorry coming so early in the day, but I've a funeral in the glen and I've been promising I'd come for so long.'

They went inside, Somerled first. He went into the living room and he saw at once that Finn was asleep in the wooden cot he had made him. Anna looked up, and her face was tired too. Her gaze flickered from the minster to her husband, as though trying to understand.

'It's good of you to come,' Somerled said, and meant it. Anna said nothing; she kept sitting where she was and waiting, as though one or the other would tell her something. Somerled saw the tight gold of the curls on her forehead, and he remembered that first day he had seen her in the inn. And he saw that she was still beautiful.

'I'm sorry to be disturbing you like this,' said John Grant softly, not wanting to waken Finn. 'I should have telephoned.'

'It's all right, John,' Anna said, and her voice was soft.

'You're welcome here, and we were glad of your kindness to my mother.'

And Somerled's heart gladdened that she had spoken as she had. She had meant to include him; at least he hoped it.

Now she got up and moved towards the two of them. 'I'll make us some tea,' she said, 'and then stay with us a bit.'

And Somerled nodded. 'Would you pray over Finn? We won't have him baptised but we'd like that. And I would have it too, for myself.'

His voice shy and soft; he felt much younger than he was.

And John Grant nodded as the first light of the young sun poured into the room, and crossed the face of the sleeping child. And the child smiled in his sleep.